Viewing Meister Eckhart
through the Bhagavad Gita

Viewing Meister Eckhart through the Bhagavad Gita

by Linda Brown Holt, D.Litt.

iUniverse, Inc.
New York Lincoln Shanghai

Viewing Meister Eckhart through the Bhagavad Gita

iUniverse, Inc.

For information address:
iUniverse, Inc.
2021 Pine Lake Road, Suite 100
Lincoln, NE 68512
www.iuniverse.com

ISBN: 0-595-32492-4 (pbk)
ISBN: 0-595-77489-X (cloth)

Contents

Acknowledgments

Are the Rhine and the Ganges so very far apart?

The miles that separate them may be less significant than the characteristics they share. The scientific, societal and even mythological properties of these two great rivers outweigh their differences in size and geography. Symbolically, they carry in their flow the cultural tides of their people, whose influences extend far beyond their course. Perhaps it is not so odd to consider the value of one in terms of the other. At least, this is the intent of this small work that views the spiritual ideas of a medieval German master through the lens of a gospel developed not far from the Ganges' shore.

Anything that is of value in this short volume on comparative spirituality has its source in the care, direction, assistance, influence, and sometimes prodding of a number of people, some of whom I've never met. These include the tireless editors of Meister Eckhart's work, from Franz Pfeiffer and C. de B. Evans, to Josef Quint (who devoted fifty years to consummate Eckhartian scholarship until his death in 1976) and Niklaus Largier (whose side-by-side, Middle High German and New High German texts were very helpful). I acknowledge my great debt to the Eckhart Society, whose members made available to me the three volumes of M. O'C. Walshe's English translation of the sermons and treatises and provided many other resources and contacts too numerous to mention. Certainly, the scholarship of Bernard McGinn, Oliver Davies, and Richard Woods, in particular, provided illumination as I approached the dense, unwieldy underbrush of Eckhart's surviving work. And I cannot omit Richard B. Blakney, the late translator of "my first Eckhart."

In the academic community, I am indebted to my undergraduate advisor, Dominic Iorio, who encouraged my interest in this subject. I greatly appreciate the vision and direction of the chair of my doctoral dissertation committee, Michael J. Christensen, Affiliate Associate Professor of Spirituality at Drew University, whose scholarly insight, enthusiasm, and creative teaching made courses on Henri Nouwen and Christian mysticism two of the most memorable experiences I had at Drew University…or anywhere. I also am indebted to Robert S. Corrington, Professor of Philosophical Theology at Drew, for sharing his insights into Eastern and Western spiritual philosophy and his ability to communicate a profound understanding of the wisdom of India in a phenomenological context. Most notably I wish to thank my understanding husband, James A. Holt, who has not let me wander from the path leading to the completion of this project, and our daughter, Vanessa Sarada Holt, for her editorial guidance.

I thank you, too, Meister Eckhart, wherever you may be. Perhaps, like the vision of Henry Suso described in the last chapter of this meditation on comparative mysticism, you look very much as you did on earth, with the addition of an otherworldly glow and a radiant demeanor of loving-kindness. At the very least, your devoted disciples have left part of your legacy for us today in the words so eloquently translated by Walshe and others. It remains an awesome thing to read, to share with people we love, and to live by.

Introduction

For more than fifty years, scholars have been struck by certain similarities in theme and practice in the works of Meister Eckhart (1260-1328), the Dominican theologian and mystic, and among many Eastern religious traditions, including the Advaita Vedanta School of Hinduism and Zen Buddhism. And yet there is no evidence that Eckhart, who taught that at some point, God and the soul are One, knew about the teachings of yogis and Zen masters. While there are good arguments that early Christian philosophy was influenced by Hinduism through Greek philosophy, it is fairly certain that Eckhart did not read or hear about the scriptures of India or the *Mahabharata*, the great Hindu epic which, like a majestic, multi-chambered shell, contains the priceless pearl of wisdom, the *Bhagavad Gita*. Dating from the 5th to 2nd century B.C.E., the *Gita* was first translated into German in the late 1700s, and would have been unknown to a Dominican scholar flourishing in Cologne and Strasburg in the High Middle Ages. But despite this separation of time and tradition, Eckhart and the anonymous author(s) of the *Bhagavad Gita* each discovered and experienced a dynamic state which they interpreted as mystical union with the Divine. They came to this state in the context of their respective philosophies, spiritual traditions, and personal practices and developed methods of communicating this to others which reveal much about the cultures and times in which they lived.

Allowing the *Gita* to guide our reading of Eckhart, we can trace the evolution of key ideas as they progress from dualism (the idea that God and the soul are two distinct entities, as implied in, "There is a point where the soul and God *become* [my italics] one") to nondualism (the empirical realization inherent in Eckhart's declaration, "God and I: we are one"). This mirrors the growth of Arjuna's consciousness as he, too, progresses from the sense that the world is two to the knowledge that Atman is Brahman: there is no separation between knower and known. The polarities of dualism and nondualism constitute a strong, unifying theme throughout this study.

Viewing Meister Eckhart through the Bhagavad Gita begins with background information about the *Gita* and Eckhart's life. A more comprehensive description of the context for the Hindu work is provided in what I hope will be considered a companion volume to this edition: the Prabhavananda-Isherwood translation of *The Song of God: Bhagavad Gita* (Hollywood: Vedanta Press, 1969).

This information is followed by reflections on four subthemes encountered in Eckhart and the *Gita:*

Dualism and Nondualism

Limited Union and Oneness with God

Pantheism and Panentheism

The Ground (*grunt* or *Grund*)

(Readers who are not particularly interested in philosophy or theology and who want to plunge right into the heart of the matter may proceed directly to the eighteen chapters if they prefer.)

The reader is then ready for a journey with the Dominican master through the eighteen chapters of the *Gita*. An appendix includes a brief collection of examples of *unitive consciousness* in world religions, a bibliography and glossary.

I hope that this book may provide insight into the universality of certain key spiritual principles while at the same time suggesting ways to examine the wisdom of both Eckhart and the *Gita* in a new light. Both works are a reminder that as our world becomes increasingly more diverse in terms of religious *practices*, our spiritual *goals* may be very much the same. How wonderful if, like Arjuna, in his final words to Krishna, at that journey's end we too may say,

By your grace, O Lord, my delusions have been dispelled.
My mind stands firm. Its doubts are ended. I will do your bidding.[1]

---

1. *Bhagavad Gita*, ed. and trans. Swami Prabhavananda and Christopher Isherwood, 3rd ed. (Hollywood, California: Vedanta Press, 1969), 173.

What is the Bhagavad Gita?

The Sanskrit narrative poem, the *Bhagavad Gita (Song of God)*, probably was composed between the fifth and second centuries B.C.E. Although it has long been part of the great Indian epic, the *Mahabharata*, scholars believe it originally was written as a separate poem by author or authors now unknown.[1]

The tale of the *Gita* unfolds on the field of Kurukshetra, a sacred place of pilgrimage, during the battle of the Pandava and Kaurava brothers following the death of the head of the dynasty, King Pandu. Describing the family relationships is a little like trying to summarize Wagner's *Ring Cycle*, so for purposes of this study, the details of this skirmish will be kept to a minimum (additional background is contained in Chapter I). Suffice it to say, there are four main speakers:

1. The blind King Dhritarashtra;

2. Sanjaya, the king's charioteer and a clairvoyant who relays events taking place on the battlefield to the king;

3. Sri Krishna, an incarnation of God and close friend, charioteer, and confident of Arjuna;

4. Arjuna, a member of the warrior caste and one of the Pandava brothers.

At the opening of the *Gita*, Dhritarashtra asks Sanjaya to tell him what is happening on the battlefield. Sanjaya then narrates the dialogue between Krishna and Arjuna that occupies most of the poem. Despite his warrior caste, Arjuna has pangs of conscience and does not want to slay his kinsmen.

---

1.   Ibid., 28.

1

Krishna, revealing his true nature as God in human form, tells Arjuna that he must perform the work for which he was born and reveals to him a series of yogas (disciplines) that will help him identify and act according to his true self. In the ensuing chapters, Krishna proceeds far beyond the scope of Arjuna's original complaint, revealing the cosmic might of the divine and outlining the path of detachment, devotion, and action that will lead all seekers to discovery of the Self which is hidden beneath appearances.

With its compelling drama, intriguing characters, and breathtaking vision, the *Gita* remains today one of the most beloved scriptures in all religious literature. Various schools of Hinduism (especially the Sankhya, Yoga, and Vedanta schools) claim the gospel as their own, and other traditions throughout the world find in its sweeping poetry a powerful articulation of the path to the knowledge of God. While not a seminal Hindu scripture *per se*, in the sense that the Vedas are authoritative, the *Gita* nonetheless has captured the hearts of billions of seekers throughout the world since it found its earliest audiences. It is a time-tested manual of spiritual development for the active man and woman of whatever era and nation. According to Aldous Huxley, the *Gita* is "…perhaps the most systematic scriptural statement of the Perennial Philosophy…pointing clearly and unmistakably to the only road of escape from the self-imposed necessity of self-destruction."[2]

---

2.   Ibid., 18-19.

Meister Eckhart:
Man, Master, and Mystic

The Dominican theologian known to the world as Meister Eckhart probably was born in the village of Tambach in the Germanic region of Thuringia in approximately 1260.[1] James M. Clark states that there is no authority for giving him the Christian name of Johannes which sometimes appears in biographical sketches. His Christian name was Eckhart; his surname was von Hochheim.[2] Eckhart was born to a noble family of landowners, but little is known about his family and early life. It appears that he joined the Dominican Order in Erfurt when he was 15, probably in 1275,[3] received orders by 1278, and was sent to continue his studies at Cologne. At that time Cologne was a renowned center of learning established by Albertus Magnus in 1248. Eckhart may have had occasion to meet or study with this elderly scholar, who taught the young Thomas Aquinas.[4] He returned to Erfurt where, it is suggested by subsequent events, that he became lector and then prior. Eckhart advanced to the University of Paris in 1293 where, at age 33, he served as a lecturer on the

1. Bernard McGinn, in *The Mystical Thought of Meister Eckhart*, (New York: Crossroad Publishing Company, 2001), 2, corrects previous scholarship which had placed Eckhart's birth in Hochheim.
2. James M. Clark, *Meister Eckhart*, (New York: Thomas Nelson and Sons Ltd., 1957), 11. McGinn also states that "von Hochheim" is a family name and does not indicate place of birth (McGinn, 3).
3. Rufus Jones, "The Mysticism of Meister Eckhart," in *At One with the Invisible*, ed. E. Hershey Sneath (New York: The MacMillan Company, 1921), 199.
4. Davies, 22.

Sentences of Peter Lombard.[5] By 1298, he had composed the earliest of his works, the *Reden der Unterscheidung*, or *Talks of Instruction* to be read aloud during meals at friaries and convents.[6] He received the honorific title, "Meister," when he completed his magistral studies in theology at the University of Paris in 1302 and assumed the external Dominican chair of theology, placing him at the apex of academic success in medieval Europe.

Eckhart was liberally educated in grammar, logic and dialectics, natural science, psychology, astronomy, metaphysics, and moral philosophy.[7] But in addition to these staples of scholasticism, he also was familiar with the vernacular and women's theological heritage of Western Europe, including the poetry of Hadewijch, the controversial writings of Marguerite Porete, and the visionary narratives of Mechtild of Magdeburg and others, by this time. In *Meister Eckhart and the Beguine Mystics*,[8] Bernard McGinn points out that in the past fifty or sixty years, scholars have come to accept the existence of three parallel theologies operating in the Middle Ages: the scholastic, the monastic (advocated by the scholar Jean LeClercq), and women's spirituality (described by the scholar Peter Dronke). While male theologians held the upper hand in Latin theology, men and women were on equal footing when it came to theology written or preached in the vernacular (German, French, etc.), according to McGinn.

By the autumn of 1303, Eckhart clearly was regarded as one of the most brilliant and charismatic theologians, preachers, and administrators in Europe.[9] When Germany (Teutonia) was divided into two provinces that year, it was to Eckhart that the Church looked for leadership of the northernmost province known as Saxonia (which included Eckhart's home area of Erfurt).[10] As Provincial, a position he held until 1311, he was responsible for 47 convents, the founding of three new Dominican houses and a host of

---

5. Richard Woods, OP, *Eckhart's Way*, (Wilmington: Michael Glazier, 1991), 28.
6. Clark, 12. McGinn thinks that its publication in the vernacular suggests it was also intended for wider distribution among the public (McGinn, 4).
7. Woods, 28.
8. Bernard McGinn, *Meister Eckhart and the Beguine Mystics*, New York: Continuum Publishing Company, 1994, 2-3.
9. McGinn, *Mystical Thought*, 5.
10. Davies, 25. Davies here is referencing J. Koch's *Kleine Schriften I*, 1973.

preaching, administrative, and diplomatic duties which took him (on foot) all over Europe.[11] During the Saxonian years, Eckhart wrote 32 Latin sermons that were posthumously included in a collection in 1340 titled, *Paradisus anime intelligentis (Paradise of the Intelligent Soul)*, which may have been intended to serve as a primer for Dominicans desiring to defend their views about the primacy of the intellect over the will (a signature Eckhartian concept).

Key ideas associated with the Meister such as God's existence beyond being and goodness, the concept of the *Ground* (*grunt* in Middle High German, *Grund* in New High German), and the eternal birth of the Word (sometimes referred to as the Son) within the Ground of the Soul, all find their genesis in the sermons of this period. Eckhart uses the word *Ground* to denote the state of being in which God is revealed directly to the seeker. He uses interchangeably the word *Abyss* to signify an infinite place beyond definition and rational knowing. Three centuries later, the German Protestant mystic Jakob Boehme would use the word *Unground* (*Ungrund*) to refer to his own understanding of that spiritual playing field, a place so beyond the reach of language and reason that he could only express what it is *not*. The concept of the *Ungrund* was taken up further in the 19th and 20th centuries by Russian theologians such as Vladimir Solovyov (1853-1900) and had a profound influence on the German romantic philosopher, G. W. F. Hegel (1770-1831) and other German Romantic philosophers (Friedrich Schelling [1775-1854] took an almost Eckhartian view, emphasizing the *Grund* rather than the *Ungrund* as synonymous with the ideal origination of Nature and the source of human consciousness).

During this period, Eckhart also wrote large sections of what he thought would be his major work, the *Opus tripartitum*, which includes his longest work, *The Commentary on the Gospel of John*. While Eckhart delivered many of his vernacular sermons while serving as Provincial, scholars have not been able to classify them according to date and place, with several exceptions (e.g., the four German sermons which compose the Christmas cycle date from the early years of this period).[12] McGinn attributes to his Provincial years the following works: the prologue to the *Book of Propositions*, his first *Commentary on Genesis*, and the *Commentary on the Book of Wisdom*.[13]

---

11. Ibid.
12. McGinn, 6. See also M.O'C. Walshe, *Meister Eckhart, Sermons & Treatises, Vol. I*, Sermons I-IV.
13. McGinn, 7.

But Eckhart's surviving output from this era provides only a slight hint as to his total achievements in his administrative and ecclesiastical leadership role. Eckhart was so successful as Saxonian Provincial that the leaders of southern Germany (known as Teutonia, the same name the undivided nation originally had held) tried to recruit him to the south. However, this invitation was interrupted when Eckhart was invited back to accept for a second time the Dominican chair in Paris, making him only the second theologian in history (after Thomas Aquinas) to be so honored.[14]

Eckhart's second tenure in Paris extended from 1311 to 1313, where, at least for a time, he resided in the same house with William of Paris, the force behind the execution of Marguerite Porete in 1310.[15] Despite his good work, Eckhart did not remain in Paris for long. Scholars are unclear as to the reason for Eckhart's departure. It may have been a combination of the Order's desire to exercise greater control over the burgeoning women's movements in the Rhineland and also Eckhart's own discomfort in the increasingly inquisitional atmosphere of Paris, where dissent could be squelched by death.

From Paris, Eckhart went on to become Vicar-General in Strasburg[16] (then part of Teutonia), a city that contained three nunneries close to the city's center (fully *half* of all Dominican convents existed in the Province of Teutonia). Strasburg was known not only for its active Dominican monastic life, but also as a center for *Beguines*, communities of lay women dedicated to prayer, poverty and good works (but who were not bound by monastic vows) and for female theology and mysticism in general. The Order, and the Church at large, looked askance at the Beguines, who, although not denying the tenets of the faith nor the authority of Rome, nonetheless encouraged independent thinking and actions that could not always be controlled. Like female mystical theologians active in monastic orders (Gertrude the Great, Mechtild of Magdeburg, and others), some of the Beguines throughout Western Europe engaged in emotional, highly visionary forms of mysticism that could, if left unmanaged, damage the integrity and authority of the Church, it was believed. Eckhart's previous success in working with nuns and other female religious, combined with his sterling character, intellect, proven leadership, and charisma, may have made him an ideal emissary to keep an eye on these

---

14. Davies, 25.
15. McGinn, 9.
16. Like Davies, 38, I use the German spelling of this city which in later years fell to the French.

trends and to prevent outbreaks of religious hysteria. Yet, how were the authorities to know the extent to which Eckhart found in the dawning of women's and vernacular theologies a mirror of some of his own most cherished convictions?

His tenure in Strasburg resulted in a number of important works, including *The Book of Divine Consolation*, dedicated to Agnes, Queen of Hungary, and *On the Noble Man*. Eckhart enjoyed ten productive years in the part of the world to which he had been wooed before his second stay in Paris. By this time, Eckhart was widely known for his unorthodox way of expressing conventional Church teachings. He spoke directly and forcefully of "higher things" to the person on the street, as well as to the most sophisticated academics and theological exegetes. He became known for his humor and down-to-earth way of speaking, his love of paradox, and imaginative use of the German language (a language he helped develop with his own trenchant yet elegant style). Above all, Eckhart's flock was drawn to him by his compassion for people and eagerness to share the most exalted thoughts with even the lowliest person. These characteristics and qualities made his discourse on religious subjects appealing, startling, and profoundly moving to diverse groups of listeners.[17]

To judge by the enthusiasm with which women's monastic and lay spiritual communities embraced the Meister and his preaching, it is safe to say that Eckhart recognized and responded positively to the work of women theologians at the end of the 13th and beginning of the 14th century. This contrib-

---

17. It is important to remember that "celebrity preachers" were almost a form of mass entertainment in the Middle Ages, providing color, fame, excitement, and the vicarious thrill of seeing and hearing people who had traveled far and wide and had spoken before Popes, royalty, and other luminaries. A popular celebrity preacher advocating a point of view contrary to that of the established Church could easily turn hundreds, even thousands of the faithful to what the Church would regard as error. It could be argued that preachers who were daring and audacious, and whose oratory titillated and provoked the average person, would be more likely to amass a following and have their message, at least at a superficial level, heard and heeded. This was certainly a concern of conservative Church leaders worried about the growth of heresies and other threats to the status quo inherent in the teachings of the Brethren of the Free Spirit, the Beguines, and their male equivalents, the Beghards.

uted, I believe, not only to the originality, vitality, and radicalism of his theology and personal practice, but also to his loss of stature as the leading Dominican theologian in Europe in the first quarter of the 14th century. For from the ashes where Porete was burned to the stake in Paris in 1310 rose the auger of Eckhart's own persecution and condemnation for heresy by a small clique of reactionaries in tune with a growing wave of inquisitional fervor in the 1320s.

His dramatic pronouncements and his enormous popularity and influence among both the religious and the laity inevitably won Eckhart many enemies. Some were the result of petty jealousies and spite, but others reflected the growing inquisitional spirit of the time, where any suggestion of heresy must be extirpated and destroyed. In 1323, Eckhart's own five-year encounter with the inquisitional Juggernaut began to unfold when he was called to the cathedral city of Cologne overseen by the man who was to be his undoing: Henry II of Virneburg, the Archbishop of Cologne.

Archbishop Henry was well known as an opponent of heresy and closely linked to Pope John XXII, at odds with the Emperor Lewis of Bavaria, who was excommunicated in 1324.[18] The archbishop already was convinced that heresy was rampant among the *Beguines*, the group so enamored of the Meister's radical teachings on the birth of the Word in the soul (without any mention of the Church's intermediary role in this process).[19] Henry's nose was sniffing the air for a big heretical rat, and who should come into his fold at this time but what was perhaps the biggest and most obvious "rat" of them all.[20] The friar who boldly preached that "God and I: we are one" and who described to the unlearned masses a path to salvation that managed to avoid mention of the sacraments and Church altogether[21] was exactly what Henry needed to make his point. Through his doing, Eckhart would become the first theologian on trial for heresy in the Middle Ages.[22]

Through Henry's influence, the Pope conducted his own investigation of Eckhart in 1325 and 1326, in which the Meister was cleared of unorthodoxy.[23] Undaunted, the archbishop prepared his own case against Eckhart in

---

18. McGinn, 14.
19. Davies, 40.
20. No pun intended on "Rat," the German word for advice or counsel.
21. Statements taken out of context, it should be emphasized.
22. McGinn, 15.
23. Ibid.

1326, resulting in Eckhart's appearance before the diocesan inquisitorial commission. Eckhart presented an eloquent *Defense* (and the trials constituted no witchhunt, for the Meister had every opportunity to present witnesses and defend himself in the courts) and had the full backing of the local Dominican authorities.[24] But, as it turned out, Eckhart won the battle but lost the war. He was not found guilty of heresy, but was summoned to the Papal court in Avignon where his case was heard by the highest earthly authority. The Meister was in his mid-sixties at the time, which would have been considered quite elderly in the Middle Ages. As a Dominican friar, he would have had to *walk* from Cologne to Avignon, a distance of some 250 miles, as monks did all their traveling on foot, making them a hearty breed.

One hundred and fifty articles of alleged heresy and other offenses were reduced to twenty-eight (twenty-six of these referred to statements from his Latin writings, two from his German works). The offending statements, taken out of context, could be interpreted as incompatible with certain views of Church dogma. In context, however, some of the statements could be seen as devices to shock lazy minds out of their complacency and to challenge people from all walks of life to think about the divine with "beginner's mind." The articles of alleged heresy included paradoxical statements from Eckhart that, taken out of context, suggest:

- The world has existed from all eternity;

- God's glory shines in all things, evil as well as good;

- The person who blasphemes against God praises God;

- That to pray *for* some benefit is actually to pray for evil;

- God is glorified in those who give up all desire;

- We are transformed into God as the communion bread is transformed into the Body of Christ;

- God loves souls, not holy works;

- A good person is the only-begotten Son of God;

---

24. Ibid.

- Everything that Holy Scripture says about Christ also is true of every just and true person;

- Every creature is "pure nothing;"

- God is neither good nor better nor best. It is false to call God "good."[25]

However, Eckhart insisted that he had always followed the essential teachings of the Church and that if he had inadvertently strayed into heresy on any point, he would completely renounce the offending doctrine. Perhaps worn out by travel, hardship, and the torment of having his personal beliefs and life's work subjected to public ridicule and condemnation, Eckhart died in Avignon, probably on Jan. 28, 1328, according to McGinn.

Not content to let Eckhart rest in peace, the Pope, undoubtedly goaded by his ally, the archbishop of Cologne, broke with tradition and, in 1329, issued the *bull* (official papal document), "In agro dominico," in which Eckhart's work was condemned posthumously. It was not until the German scholar Franz Pfeiffer issued an edition of Eckhart's work in 1857[26] that the leading Dominican master of his time and one of the most brilliant mystical theologians of all time, returned to the attention of the public he so loved and desired to serve.

The ideas Eckhart expresses in the German-language sermons and texts with which he communicated with his colleagues and countrymen contain a number of subthemes which have intrigued scholars and laypeople alike through the centuries. Four of the most significant subthemes are explored in the following section.

---

25. Examples extracted from M. O'C. Walshe, "Articles Condemned in the Bull of John XXII," in *Meister Eckhart, Sermons & Treatises, Vol. 1* by Meister Eckhart, trans. M.O'C. Walshe (Longmead, Shaftsbury: Element Books Limited, 1987), xlvii-li.
26. Davies, 13.

Four Subthemes in Eckhart and the Gita

The gist of this study can be described in few words; to wit, we can learn much about the mystical theology of Meister Eckhart by viewing his works through the lens of the *Bhagavad Gita*. The *Gita* gives us a framework for viewing and considering Eckhart's ideas about the nature of God, the relationship of individual soul to the divine, and the path to knowing and experiencing "our original face, before we were born," to use a phrase from a Zen *koan* (see Glossary). This framework succeeds because it provides a perspective outside the conventions and limitations of Western European thought. By viewing Eckhart in this context, we observe universal patterns, concepts, and conclusions that link the Meister's insights to the wisdom body of other nations and other times, while observing distinctions that make his contributions to world mysticism unique and meaningful.

In demonstrating this thesis, four subthemes run as an undercurrent throughout the German works of Eckhart as viewed through the *Gita*. Three of these subthemes consist of pairs of polar opposites, challenging us to question our assumptions. These subtheme pairs are: *dualism* and *nondualism*; *limited union* and *Oneness with God*; and *pantheism* and *panentheism*. The fourth subtheme is one grand concept: the *Grund* (*grunt* in the German of Eckhart's day) or *Ground*, a concept which in various permutations influenced the ensuing history of Western philosophy and theology at least until our time.

How does the *Gita* help us clarify and understand these elements? In its role as a lens and organizing device, the *Gita* allows us to experience these ideas as dynamic energy. Like electrical currents flashing back and forth between positive and negative poles, their substance is in the force they release through movement rather than in their static locus at either extreme. To push

11

the metaphor even further, their substance exists not in the thing itself, but in the way our mind perceives and responds to this *kinesis*.

In order to appreciate this fully, we need to understand what these opposite conditions are, and how they relate to each other in the quest for spiritual understanding.

Dualism and Nondualism

Dualism, or the ultimate lack of unity of all things, is a common theme that appears in both the *Gita* and the works of Meister Eckhart. Dualists hold that God is utterly separate from and ultimately unknowable to humanity, or, at the very least, God and humanity may co-exist in separate realms which may intersect. Monists claim there is, in essence (ontologically), no ultimate distinction between human and divine. Most thinkers and believers fall somewhere in between on the spectrum, settling for an uneasy oscillation between these two absolute poles. For some, consciousness may move from one perspective to the other, and perhaps back again (i.e., one may experience momentary union during prayer, but a sense of the distinctions between matter and spirit while at work or with family).

Lao Tzu, the originator of philosophical Taoism, states that the newborn child is in perfect harmony with the *Tao*, the Chinese word for the ultimate nature of being, but through conditioning and training, becomes separate, estranged from the "Mother of the 10,000 things." Gautama the Buddha said that our original mind is clear and shining, but it is sullied through ignorance and estrangement from our pure nature. Scientists such as Nobel Laureate Roger Sperry have speculated that the human brain once was a unified network of intellect and intuition that snapped into two halves in prehistoric times, creating disharmony, a yearning for reconciliation. Classical Christian doctrine teaches that God and human shared one perfect harmony before *the Fall*. After the introduction of sin into the world, divine intervention of a Savior was required—God's incarnation in the material world—to restore humanity to original grace. *Saddhus* (holy men and women) of India believe we are bound by the chains of *samsara* at birth, and must engage in religious and spiritual practices and austerities throughout life in order to restore harmony and achieve a state of union with God. While some believers think Jesus's words, "I and the Father are one," were evidence of his unique divinity, others have concluded that the carpenter's son was instructing people to experience this unity for themselves.

In addition to the dualism of God and humanity, there are other dualisms at play in a religious worldview. There is God versus nature, for example, and most notably, good versus evil. Western religions with their roots in the Middle East tend to view good and evil as irreconcilably dualistic in nature. Good is what is in accord with God, evil is the work of the devil. And yet Satan is not the equal of God, though evil works may appear to overwhelm the appearance of good in the world. In contrast, one often finds in Eastern faith traditions a less adversarial view of good and evil. In Hinduism, evil is the result of *avidya*, or ignorance. As one engages in spiritual activities, including service to others, and studies and learns the truth, which is Brahman, evil dissolves into its true nature: illusion. In Taoism, evil and good are two halves of the same coin, the *t'ai chi* of opposites (a concept not dissimilar to a conclusion reached by Baruch de Spinoza). As long as one is caught in the force field of dualism, he or she will not experience the unified state of knowledge beyond opposites which is the *Tao*. By focusing on the *Tao*, practitioners assert that one rises beyond superficial notions of good and evil and enters a profound understanding and experience of the highest Good.

However, East and West also contain seeds of the other, like the *t'ai chi* symbol, which contains a black half and a white half, each containing a seed of the other:

Certainly, believers in the East have done battle with the forces of darkness, no matter how elevated their consciousness, while many in the West have achieved enlightened states allegedly beyond good and evil, comparable to those of Eastern *rishis* (Indian saints) and *shens* (enlightened Taoists).

Certainly, the concept of union with the divine has generated controversy since the establishment of many of the world's major religious traditions. The ideal of union with God inspires and motivates many on the spiritual quest. However, others, especially those in the reputedly more rational West, recoil from these words with horror or dismiss them sardonically as pantheism. Among believers, union with God may refer to a state of return to original harmony, as in Taoism or Buddhism, or the progression from dualism to non-distinction. For others, it may represent a progression from a sense of separation (as in original sin) to reconciliation. For many seekers (notably in the various schools of Buddhism), it is a matter of learning to see clearly the Reality that has always been, so to speak, right under one's nose.

Just as there are different ways of thinking about the *Ground*, there are several schemes for approaching the concept of dualism. It is not only God and human that may seem to be separate from one another. The history of philosophy and religion rings with the clash of opposites: God versus nature, nature versus nurture, good versus evil. The problem of evil is an issue of dualism. In Western traditions, evil is a force opposed to God/good, *but the devil is not equal to God*, simply a fallen angel with an enormous amount of influence (not unlike a computer virus). In the East, evil may more often than not be viewed as ignorance (*avidya* in Hinduism), while in Taoism good-and-evil is one of the endless pairings of opposites that characterize the phenomenal world. When one experiences and understands the union of individual self and universal Self, one *transcends* (and *implends*[1]) good and evil and *attains* (or recaptures) a state of harmony where distinctions of this type dissolve. Critics, particularly in the West, are loath to accept the idea that people can rise beyond good and evil, citing mystical Nazism and the Taliban as examples of what happens when people believe their spiritual destiny elevates them beyond the mass of humanity. However, even a cursory reading of the sacred scriptures and testimonials of mystics of the world's major faiths reveals that nothing of the sort is recommended. The search for union is not the proper quest of the elite, but a path each person may follow to discover for him or herself the true meaning of life and ground of being.

Another form of dualism linked to the search for union is the association of spirituality with sensuality, and mystical ecstasy with sexual rapture. Certainly, there are few more apt metaphors for the soul's journey toward God than the attraction of male and female culminating in sensual union. In Taoism, the metaphor is extended even to the point of conception, where a "spiritual

---

1. In the spirit of dualism, I have created the neologism, "implend," to balance the meaning of the word, "transcends." *Transcend* suggests going beyond, past and across to attain something higher and more rarified. *Implends* means leaving the world of phenomena and going within, deeper into a state not unlike implosion where meaning becomes evident by turning in on itself.

embryo" is developed during meditation which in time will yield "the red baby"[2] (realization and oneness with the *Ground*). In certain Taoist practices (not mainstream, to be sure, but common enough throughout history), the spiritual search is emulated and (it is believed) enhanced by complementary sexual activity following a prescribed formula.[3] Hinduism as well offers a sexual path to spiritual bliss as part of its *tantric* tradition,[4] while Islam, through the mystical path of Sufism, offers a rich heritage of erotic poetry (of which *The Rubaiyat* is a mild example) as a metaphor for the ineffable experience of union with Allah. Judaism expressed the yearning for sensual oneness in the *Song of Songs*. The *Beguines* of medieval Christianity (communities of lay women dedicated to meditation, prayer and good works) expressed their passion for Jesus in erotic *Brautmystik* poetry and narratives, in which the soul and Christ were depicted as bride and groom. These expressions have led some psychologists to brand religious fervor as nothing more than sublimated sexuality. But this is reductionistic. Is there is anything in human experience closer in feeling and intensity to the search for mystical union than the hunger for sensual consummation? One simply cannot imagine a more convincing metaphor (the hunger for lunch, for example, just doesn't compare). And yet the erotic metaphor remains in essence a dualist model.

Finally, a form of dualism shared by mystics East and West is the concept of flow. This is best illustrated by the circuit formed by two single-cell batteries with positive and negative poles. The current flows continuously from one to the other in a kind of Möbius-strip circuit. There is dualism in the existence of the positive and negative poles, but at the same time there is nondualism in the invisible but powerful current of energy that their tension releases. This idea of *flow* is an important concept not only in the work of Meister Eckhart, but also in the meditation practices of *kundalini yoga* and the micro-and macro-cosmic orbit meditations of Taoism (in brief, the yogic practice focuses

---

2.   See Chang Po-Tuan, *The Inner Teachings of Taoism* trans. Thomas Cleary with commentary by Liu I-Ming, (Boston: Shambhala Press, 1986).

3.   For a discussion of Taoist *tantra* in a fictional setting, see Simone Marnier, *White Tiger, Green Dragon* (New York: Author's Choice Press, 2000).

4.   Tantra is a yogic path that uses the senses and one's experience of the phenomenal world as a vehicle to attain enlightenment.

on flow from bottom to top, while the Taoist technique emphasizes a continuous circle of energy).

Of course, the *Gita* is open to interpretation through all of these perspectives, both dualist and nondualist alike. There are, in fact, many compelling reasons for reading the *Gita* as a dualist tract. From the onset, Arjuna is positioned as a limited mortal while Krishna is cast in the role of infinite Other. There is no doubt that the world as viewed from the plain at Kurukshetra is quite a different place from the spectacular realm of God depicted in Chapter X. Dualism pervades the *Gita*: Arjuna is ignorant, Krishna is wise; attachment to sensual pleasures leads to delusion, while surrender to the divine will leads to bliss; and so forth.

Yoga, one of the six schools of Hinduism, tends to support a dualist reading of the *Gita*, pitting limited worldly life against the deity's awesome power. According to this view, humanity and deity are separate. Limited union may occur only when the inferior self submits to the vastly superior Self.

Vedanta, generally regarded as the most profound and esoteric school of Hinduism, teaches that we are already God. Like the angel who greets visitors to Jesus's empty tomb, Vedanta seems to ask, "Why seek the living among the dead?" God is here, alive, and *you are That.* However, deluded by appearances and delusion, humanity does not see the forest for the trees, does not recognize that its own essential nature is identical to the essence of God. Education is the broom that sweeps away the dust of illusion, the cobwebs of ignorance, to help us see and experience what is *real.* In this reading of the *Gita*, there is no difference between the substance of self and Self. They are the same, but may be viewed differently, as in the optical illusion below:

Is this a picture of a white chalice on a black background, or of two black profiles on a white background? Or, ultimately, is this a square containing both in the form of a black-and-white design?

In using the *Gita* as a kind of searchlight to illuminate the works of Eckhart, I favor the nondualist approach. This is because mystics throughout history and across cultures have agreed that dualism is somehow incomplete, that we must push further and learn to see Reality with eyes unconditioned by culturally inculcated norms of "this" versus "that." God is one, and through meditation, we realize our own participation in that Oneness, though to what degree this nondualism extends differs depending on the religious environment, spiritual practices (such as meditation) undertaken, and how far the mystic is willing or able to proceed. I accept this nondualist view of the *Gita*, however, with one modification. This modification is an emphasis on the *progression* from a dualist to a nondualist perspective. In a sense Eckhart and the *Gita* reflect *both* dualist and nondualist approaches. Depending on how one looks at it, Yoga and Vedanta are both correct. What intrigues me, however, is how the "thought of two" flows into or evolves into the "idea of One." Both texts outline the movement of consciousness from the "I-Thou" to the "I am That" state, describing a pathway to the "Oh, I get it!" experience when what seemed to be two reveals itself unequivocally as One.

The *Gita* begins with a premise of separation and provides a model of education, a course of training ostensibly to lead to the realization of Oneness with God. This union reflects a state of *homoousion* (same substance), to import a Christian theological term that the Council of Nicea used to describe the nature of Christ (simultaneously fully God and fully human). And so, according to a nondualist reading of the *Gita*, we each have the potential to become Christs in the sense of having the same substance as God.

Such a statement would seem heretical to some Christians, and indeed, charges of heresy were aimed at Meister Eckhart for making just this kind of declaration. But with Eckhart as well as the *Gita*, the realization is grounded in the orthodox[5] position that humans may know God, and that in order to

---

5.   Taken out of context, many of Meister Eckhart's sayings seem heterodox ("God and I: we are one," for example). However, some of the deliberately unsettling statements he made were ensconced in declarations and teaching that were conventional and didactic in substance and tone. Throughout his life and ministry, Eckhart was regarded by Church leadership, colleagues, and students alike as a model Christian and defender of Church doctrine, witness his ever-growing range of responsibilities and academic reputation. However, he made a certain number of enemies because of his outspokenness and use of colorful metaphors, and one of these (see Introduction-Part I) had the ear of the burgeoning Inquisition, which led to charges of heresy toward the end of his life.

know fully, we must to some degree be united with the object of knowledge. This nondualism is based on a union which is not sameness. "God" and "human" are not identical, interchangeable terms. Yet the nondualist would aver that the substance of their essential nature is one. According to this holistic point of view, estranged people who do not recognize this union feel like foreigners in far places when in fact they are always at home. It is the goal of masters such as Eckhart and the author of the *Gita* to help them wake up and experience their participation in the Eternal Now.

In this context, the *Gita* is a useful tool for exploring the directions of Eckhart's efforts to help men and women recognize and experience their own participation in the divine. The *Gita* enables us to view Eckhart's work[6] in a fresh light, challenging us to compare and contrast the path to union with the divine as described more than 2,000 years ago in a small section of the epic *Mahabharata* with the Meister's observations and experiences shared with monastics, lay religious, and "everyday people" in Germany and France in the 13th and 14th centuries. Both Eckhart and the anonymous author of the *Gita* struggle with the stranglehold with which dualism grips the world. But while each provides a similar process for breaking the chains which keep humanity from divine understanding, they approach their subject quite differently, as differently, in fact, as two sources of the same truth could be. These two bodies of work—one Eastern, the other Western; one by an anonymous author or authors, the other by a high-profile academician and popular preacher; one from the Golden Age of India, the other from the European high middle ages—work together, explicate each other, and tell us something profound about the universality of the search for God. Viewing the one (Meister Eckhart) through the other (the *Gita*) will prove to be an intriguing and possibly serendipitous adventure for anyone hoping to understand a path to union which crosses boundaries of time, place and tradition.

---

6.   This study focuses primarily on the vernacular sermons which present the Meister's ideas to both monastic and lay audiences.

Limited Union and Oneness with God

Through the ages, Christians have tended to be uncomfortable with the idea of union with God. There is no doubt that the Christian scriptures can be read purely from a dualist perspective. According to this view, God is "up there," humanity is "down here," and while the twain may meet, they will never be the same, at any level.

Christian mystics and their defenders, however, think differently. Those seeking the inward path from the early days of Origen, Maximus the Confessor and Clement of Alexandria, to the medieval mystics, on to contemplative philosophers like Vladimir Solovyov, Simone Weil, and Brother David Stendl-Rast, have suggested (and sometimes stated flat out) that there is common ground shared by the human soul and the divine. Their viewpoint is based in part on sound philosophical analysis, careful reading of scriptures, and, in no small part, on personal practice and experience.

There are two major camps among those who support the idea that God and humanity can be united, at least to some degree. The first is the camp of limited union, those for whom the soul is fundamentally different from God, but at times does share sweet moments of unity in which God's being and human being can merge. Followers of this camp include mystics such as Teresa of Avila, a 16th century Spanish Carmelite nun, Roman Catholic saint, and Doctor of the Church, whose heart was "wounded" by the arrows of divine love.

> For He has been pleased to unite Himself with His creature in such a way that they have become like two who cannot be separated from one another: even so He will not separate Himself from her.[7]

Blaise Pascal, the 17th century French mathematician and philosopher, wrote of being "on fire" with divine union, but did not suggest that he was one with God in any permanent sense.

The second is the realm of those who believe that the substance or essential being of the divine is *exactly the same* as the substance of the soul. In fact, it is only ignorance born of delusion that keeps people from recognizing this as fact, these believers declare. This is the view of Vedanta, one of the six schools

---

7.   Teresa of Avila, *Interior Castle*, trans. E. Allison Peers (New York: Bantam Doubleday Dell Publishing Group, 1990), 213-214.

of Hindu philosophy, which teaches *Brahman* (the Godhead, or God in the most abstract sense) and *Atman* (the soul) are one. In a similar spirit, Buddhism cries, "Wake up! End the cycle of craving that binds you to this illusory world. Open your eyes, and see!" Many Christians, too, also claim to have awakened to this profound realization. "God's love and mine converged," wrote Blessed Angela of Foligno (1248-1309), a professed Member of the Third Order of St. Francis. At times, God seems to say to Angela, "You are I, and I am you."[8] Nicholas of Cusa, a papal advisor in 15th century Italy, wrote, "...in you the finite is united to the infinite and to that which cannot be united, and the incomprehensible is seized by an eternal fruition, which is a most joyous and inexhaustible happiness."[9]

In my opinion, this common ground extends to the views of mystical union advanced in Meister Eckhart's German works and the *Gita*. The *Gita*, like Eckhart in his *Talks of Instruction*, begins with a limited view of union. Arjuna is *in* the chariot, but Krishna is the charioteer. Similarly, Eckhart's early teachings emphasize obedience and conformity above personal quest. However, by the end of the *Gita*, Krishna has invited Arjuna (as Everyman/woman) to become immersed in the Godhead. Eckhart, too, in his later works, goes so far as to suggest that vows and rules are means to an end when that end is union with God. Once one has savored the sweet taste of union, disciplines fall aside, like crutches no longer needed. Unity then becomes a matter of substance in the here and now, a living, experiential reality, not a theoretical abstraction lurking in some unforeseeable tomorrow.

But does this mean that God is *in* everything, or simply that everything is God? That is a question broached by the next pair of opposites: *pantheism* and *panentheism*.

---

8. Angela of Foligno, *Angela of Foligno: Complete Works* (Mahwah, New Jersey: Paulist Press, 1993), 183, 205.
9. *Nicholas of Cusa: Selected Spiritual Writings*, trans. Hugh Lawrence Bond (Mahwah, New Jersey: Paulist Press, 1997), 278.

Pantheism and Panentheism

Can temporal duality and ultimate unity coexist? Indeed, is it possible that they can interpenetrate and nourish each other? After viewing the ideas of Meister Eckhart as seen through the *Gita*, I am convinced that these two states of being not only exist, but also form a system of "flow" in individuals and peoples open to an experience of being that is richer than day-to-day existence. Certainly, in order to function in the everyday world, men and women must deal with the demands of a dualistic universe. That dualism may be expressed in the divide between human and divine, or in the way we define reality through pairs of opposites (e.g., good and evil, light and dark, day and night). Every mystic and seer, no matter how sheltered from the "world of dust," as the Taoists refer to phenomenal existence, must deal with these opposites every day. No matter how tightly we close the doors of the senses, at some point we have to decide to eat or to go hungry, to sleep or to stay awake, to speak out against injustice or to remain silent. These choices are relentless, and yet, in the midst of these "terrible two's," comes the sweeping vision of connectedness that illumines seekers (and those in their presence) like golden sunshine slicing through a rain-weary sky. It might last a moment or sustain an enlightened spirit through a lifetime (and possibly beyond). But at some point, the mystic is able to function simultaneously in the world of the senses *and* the Ground of All Being. Only for the mystic, there's no "*and*" about it: the flow is undivided, and the knowledge is One.

Nonetheless, a view of mystical knowledge as a process of spiritual flow can be troubling. Somehow, it is easier to imagine the soul flowing back to the Source of All Being than to imagine God "coming down" to the level of human nature. And yet that is exactly the message of the Hindu and Christian gospels. We are not simply "dewdrops melting in the shining sea," to use Sir Edwin Arnold's elegant phrase. The "Sea," as it were, takes the form of the "dewdrop," as God becomes Krishna or Christ in a confused, befuddled world. "God became human so that human may become divine."[10]

This is what Eckhart means when he talks so enthusiastically, but, for many readers today, so enigmatically about the eternal Birth of the Son in the Ground of the Soul. The flow is always taking place, like the macro-cosmic

---

10. Jakob Boehme quoting Athanasius in *The Way of Christ*, trans. Peter Erb, *The Classics of Western Spirituality*, (New York, Mahwah: Paulist Press, 1978).

orbit in Taoist meditation, a process whereby the seeker visualizes the flow of a golden energy current up the front of the body, over the head, down the back and up the front again and again. And the flow is not, from a dualist's perspective, one-sided. God needs the human soul as much as the human soul needs God. In fact, Eckhart says, "God would die without humanity!" (paraphrased from Sermon 83, Walshe). What an astonishing statement! In my opinion, this is true *panentheism*, the view that God permeates all, like water dispersed throughout a damp beach towel. The twentieth-century American philosopher Charles Hartshorne coined the term, *panentheism*, for his development of a concept that originated in the work of Alfred N. Whitehead. *Panentheism* is different than *pantheism*, the philosophical and religious position that the world is identical with God or expresses the nature of God. *Pantheism* has a distinguished history in spirituality and philosophy, with its proponents claiming that the teachings of Plato, Spinoza, Thoreau and the Vedanta of India are in essence pantheistic philosophies. On the other hand, *Panentheism* tells us that God is *in* everything, but *not* everything. *Panentheism* is a dynamic process grander than the birth and death of stars, more intimate than the coming and going of our breath. *Panentheism* shows us that getting there is half the fun (and maybe the whole thing). When two become one in process, they become *one* in essence. Period. So, for Eckhart, as for the ecstatic narrator of the *Gita*, there is nothing paranormal or supernatural about the mystical quest for the divine. It is simply a matter of discovering what has always been right under our nose, "the face we wore before we were born" (to quote a Zen *koan*). When we realize (often in a sudden, defining moment) that we've been looking at life the wrong way, then all the galaxies shine like mandalas and the words flowing from our lips swell to the heavens like unknown tongues.

Such a cacophony it creates, like the roar of a flock of grackles overhead as they blacken the sky. But is there a way to deal with this wild, all-consuming knowledge, to organize and to take it in bite-size pieces the mind can comprehend? The structure and predictability of the form may be the answer, making the ethereal content comprehensible. The rapture shines through purposefully, radiance filtered through panels of stained glass. This is how the eighteen chapters of the *Gita* may help us grab hold of Meister Eckhart's soaring ideas. As the Meister himself said of our pursuit of God, "...we need to be able to sneak up on Him and throw a towel over Him to grab God naked in all His Truth." In addition to its peerless stature as a tool for self-transformation, the *Gita* also gives us the power to see Eckhart in this shining light and to digest the ideas that dissolve all ignorance away.

The Ground (grunt or Grund)

Meister Eckhart was not the first theologian or mystic to use the word *Ground* to describe the playing field where spiritual experience unfolds. But he was the first to make *Ground* the keystone to his philosophy. According to McGinn, "it is in the works of Eckhart that the word first achieves centrality as a way of presenting mystical consciousness."[11] This is not to say that *Ground* was relegated to minor status by the originators of the Christian theological traditions (east and west). The hermetic *Book of the Twenty-four Philosophers* which states, in a sentence frequently mistakenly attributed to Eckhart, "God is the infinite sphere whose center is everywhere and whose circumference is nowhere,"[12] affirms the notion of *Ground* without using the term *per se*.[13] The dimension of God[14] defined in this statement presages Eckhart's concept of *Ground* as the source of all being, the place where human soul and infinite Godhead intersect and share the same nature. This is a very deep wellspring hidden in every human soul, and the one thing that gives human life profound significance and meaning. The *Ground* is the undifferentiated Godhead, all that is core and central to the nature of being. But we, according to Eckhart, are not aliens shanghaied on a planet out of God's grasp. A spark of the divine nature lurks in each person, and, if sought and allowed to catch fire, enables us to understand and commune with the divine as with our deepest self.

The spiritual seeker who would get to the *Ground* first must pass through the valley of detachment and cross the desert that lies between intoxication with the illusory world of the senses and the frank apprehension of the essence of all that truly is.[15] Mystics before Eckhart tended to get stuck in the equation of detachment with deprivation. Because of this, we find Mechtild of Magdeburg using *abgrunt* in the negative sense of hell, even the rapturous

---

11. McGinn, 40.
12. Quoted in McGinn, 38
13. It also sounds a bit like a 21st century physicist's concept of the Universe.
14. Other dimensions would be God as love, God incarnate, God as wisdom, et. al.
15. When I think of the mystic seeker at this stage, I envision T.E. Lawrence as portrayed by Peter O'Toole in *Lawrence of Arabia*. Specifically, it is the moment when he looks out across the impassable desert known as "the Devil's Anvil," and setting his jaw firmly, resolves to conquer this formidable obstacle in pursuit of his dream.

Hadewijch speaking of *afgront* or the abyss as the moment of interpenetration of God and human soul in unitive bliss.[16] But McGinn notes that when it appears in Eckhart, *abgrunt* is of secondary significance; it is *grunt*—the affirmative essence of all being—which is the central metaphor.[17]

While remaining true to the spirit of early Christianity, *grunt* is also different from earlier concepts of the divine *milieu* linguistically: it is a purely Germanic word. McGinn, who more than any other scholar has written extensively of the importance of this concept in Eckhart's theology, notes that there is no exact equivalent in Latin, the language of the world of western spirituality in which Eckhart moved. Other terms appearing in Eckhart's Latin works (*fundis animae, apex mentis, ratio superior,* et. al.) are associated with the mysticism of introversion and find their source in the work of Augustine of Hippo, McGinn avers.[18] In part, this is true because Eckhart found in his own tongue the nuances necessary to describe Reality in a new, fresh way, liberated from conventional Latin terms. This may be one reason why his vernacular writings pop off the page at us today—challenging and vigorous—while the more measured phrases translated from Latin present an intellectually convincing but emotionally constrained pedagogy.

McGinn points out that there are actually four different meanings to *grunt*—two concrete and two abstract—in Middle High German. *Grunt* may mean a physical ground or place, as well as the bottom of a body or structure. These two meanings do not occur in Eckhart. Abstractly, *grunt* may suggest origin, cause, and beginning; or the hidden essence. It is this latter definition, linked to the Meister's dynamic concept of flow, that forms the matrix for his mystical theology.[19]

Viewing the Meister's German sermons and writings through the lens of the *Gita*, it is not so difficult to see a kinship between the *grunt* and the *Self* of Advaita Vedanta. Both suggest a ground of all Being, a hidden essence revealed to those who would still mind and senses, and look deeply for the true meaning of life. Both declare that essential Being is a flowing, dynamic process rather than a static object. Both claim that *Ground* and *Self* may be known through the mind, the soul, and the loving heart. And while acknowledging a dualist worldview in the early stages of the development of consciousness,

16. McGinn, 44.
17. Ibid.
18. McGinn, 41.
19. McGinn, 42

both claim that the spiritual seeker ultimately will recognize life in the *Ground* as a unified state of being where God and man intersect and interpenetrate.

The eighteen chapters of Gita in themselves tell the story in its entirety and lead us to a clearer understanding of Eckhart's progression from dualist Paris master to fearless prophet of unitive consciousness.

1

The Sorrows of Arjuna

The eighteen chapters of the *Bhagavad Gita* comprise chapters 25 through 42 in the Hindu epic, the *Mahabharata*. The epic traces the adventures of two families, those of Pandu (the Pandavas) and his brother, the blind king Dhritarashtra (the Kauravas). Pandu inherited the ancestral lands in northern India (near what is today New Delhi), but died, leaving his five sons—including his son Arjuna—in the keeping of their uncle, who, despite his visual infirmity, managed to sire 100 sons of his own. The epic extols the virtues of the five Pandavas while excoriating the 100 Kauravas as a scurrilous lot of rascals, rogues, and reprobates.

When the worst of the Kaurava clan gets the upper hand, the five Pandavas are exiled to the forest. When they return to claim their inheritance, war erupts involving not only the family, but everyone throughout the realm. As befits a virtuous hero, Arjuna obtains as his personal charioteer Lord Krishna, an incarnation of God. Far from the battlefield, the legendary Hindu sage Vyasa provides a clairvoyant reporter named Sanjaya to the blind king Dhritarashtra to help him stay in touch with breaking news. Through Sanjaya's clairvoyance, Dhritarashtra hears the narrative of the *Gita* as it unfolds in dialogue between the hesitant Arjuna and the divine avatar holding his chariot's reins.

Stated in Chapter I of the *Gita*, the sorrows of Arjuna are the lamentations of humanity. "Who am I? What is my duty? How can I resolve conflict?" Foreshadowing Hamlet, Arjuna is humanity divided, like the bicameral brain, into two halves: a half of contemplation where dreams, theoretical questioning, and imagination hold sway, and a half of action, dominated by duty,

28

immediacy, and decisiveness. When the *Gita* opens on the plain of Kurukshetra, Arjuna cannot break loose from the questions that arise and flicker
through his consciousness. He is caught in a terrible pause, like a Victrola needle annoyingly stuck in a record's groove, and cannot resolve his dilemma and
propel himself into the field of activity. His duty as a member of the warrior
class is to do battle, but herein (as Hamlet would say) lies the rub. For to
engage in this particular battle with the Kuntis is to attack and slay his kinsmen, the cousins and nephews and teachers he has known personally or by
repute since his earliest years. "Far better would it be for me if the sons of
Dhritarashstra, weapons in hand, should slay me in the battle, unarmed and
unresisting," said Arjuna. Having spoken thus on the battlefield, notes the
narrator Sanjaya, Arjuna "cast aside his bow and arrow and sank down on his
chariot-seat, his mind overcome with grief."[1]

Arjuna is stuck, not on the plain of Kurukshetra, but on the plain of the
phenomenal world where duty and honor are the most important values,[2] different in intensity and character than their equivalent concepts in both the
Western medieval and contemporary worlds. Arjuna's dilemma is preemi-
nently the suffering of a soul caught in the grinding jaws of dualism, and at
this point, it is Eckhart who can shed light on the *Gita*'s opening conundrum.

"People often say, 'Pray for me,'" said Eckhart in one of his vernacular sermons. When these petitioners say "pray for me," they are creating a distinction
not only between themselves and the Meister, but also between themselves
and the divine source. "And I think (to myself)," he continues, "'Why do you
go out? Why do you not stay within yourself and draw on your own treasure?[3]
For you have the whole truth in its essence within you.'"[4]

While duty has a different meaning for Eckhart, he clearly was a man of
weighty responsibilities, who lived in a world dominated by order. Hindu
society was based on castes and hierarchies which the ecclesiastical leaders of
the time believed were divinely ordained. Not dissimilarly, as a Dominican
friar, provincial, and vicar with enormous responsibilities in terms of people

1. *Bhagavad Gita*, trans. Swami Nikhilananda (New York: Ramakrishna-
    Vivekananda Center, 1987), 1:46-47.
2. Sri Aurobindo, *The Bhagavad Gita and its Message*, (Twin Lakes, Wis-
    consin: Lotus Light Publications, 1995), 16 footnote.
3. That is to say, divine essence, that part of the self where soul, according
    to Eckhart, is blessed to be united with God.
4. Eckhart, Sermon 13, *Sermons and Treatises*, 1:119.

and property, Eckhart lived in a highly regulated subset of a medieval society dominated by the Roman Church. While it is true that the Meister himself was no physical warrior, there still would be—in fact, *were*—times when his obedience to the religious powers of his time would result in actions, including deaths,[5] which he undoubtedly viewed with a revulsion tantamount to Arjuna's.

Certainly, there are limits to how far the comparison between the 14th century Dominican and the mythic hero from India's Golden Age can hold, but it would be naïve to think that Eckhart as a monastic was protected and immune from the kind of painful life-and-death decision making Arjuna describes in his opening soliloquy. Through the window of the *Gita*, we can focus on and understand Eckhart's experience and empathy, and note that the direction to seek unitive knowledge which he recommends is in fact a path parallel to the *Gita*'s to overcoming confusion, transcending suffering, and understanding the meaning of life. The dualism that Krishna will identify as the heart of Arjuna's and humanity's malaise is the same obstacle that prevents what Eckhart terms "the eternal birth of the Word in the Ground of the Soul."[6] In the words of the Meister, "The blessed see God in a single image, and in that image, they discern all things. God too sees Himself thus, perceiving all things in Himself."[7]

---

5.   I am thinking of the martyrdoms of dissidents such as Porete. Eckhart's preaching and writing are unified in their reasonableness, containing nothing to suggest support of executions and other inquisitional activities.

6.   "...wa got der vater spreche sin wort in der sele (where God the Father speaks his Word in the soul)..." Eckhart, Sermon 1, *Sermons, 1:19-20*. The location of this speaking is identified as the *grunt* (*ground*), "the purest thing that the soul is capable of, in the noblest part..." Ibid., 3. This is a technical usage of the word *grunt* by Eckhart for the essence of the soul where it is one with God. This is a different usage than the reference to God as the Ground of All Being, the Tao, or some other synonym for the divine, as mentioned in the first footnote to this chapter.

7.   Ibid., Sermon 2, 20.

2

The Yoga of Knowledge

Responding to the dejected warrior, Krishna begins his discourse of revelation regarding the meaning of life. First, he reveals to Arjuna the way that can be known through the intellect, expressing a view of an eternal God and immortal souls which, except for the doctrine of reincarnation, is not dissimilar to traditional Christian doctrine. There was never a time when God and the soul did not exist, nor will there be such a time in the future.[1] "Bodies are said to die, but That which possesses the body is eternal. It cannot be limited, or destroyed."[2] Krishna appeals to Arjuna to use his intellect to discover the evidence for this revelation.

For Eckhart, too, *intellect* is all. But not simply intellect as we normally think of it. Everyday mind (*nous*) is but a point of entry to the All-Mind which is God. Eckhart's perspective is not unlike that of the Vedantist[3] for whom the small *self* is a pale foreshadowing of the mighty *Self* at the heart of

---

1. *Bhagavad Gita*, trans. Annie Besant, 18th ed., (Wheaton, Ill.: Theosophical Publishing House, 2000), 2:12.
2. *Bhagavad Gita*, trans. Prabhavananda and Isherwood, 40.
3. Sri Aurobindo states that the "*Gita* is in its foundation a Vedantic work; it is one the three recognized authorities for the Vedantic teaching." *Gita*, trans. Aurobindo, 27.

all being.[4] Reflecting his Platonic roots, Eckhart views knowledge not as a collection of facts or mental processes, but rather the core of all being. God is perfect knowing, and to know God is to share in His divinity. "...the eternal Word is spoken inwardly, in the heart of the soul, in the inmost and purest, in the head of the soul of which I just spoke, in the intellect, and therein the birth takes place."[5]

In East and West, if intellect (from the Latin, *intelligere*, to know) is the process, then knowledge (from the Greek, *gnosis*, knowledge as subject or predicate) is the content. In Hinduism, knowledge has several different meanings. In Nyaya, one of the six major schools of Hindu philosophy, knowledge (or *jnana*) is "a product that arises from the contact of the self with the mind, or from the connection of the self, the mind, the sense-organ, and the object."[6] In contrast, Advaita Vedanta, often held to be the highest form of Hindu philosophy, and certainly the most abstract, holds that knowledge is primarily, "Pure Consciousness."[7] But before he can teach Arjuna about the knowledge of consciousness beyond dualism, Krishna introduces a theme

---

4. This point of view was developed independently in the middle of the 19th century by Mary Baker Eddy who was familiar with neither the tenets of esoteric Hinduism (except as filtered through the influence of New England Transcendentalism) nor the work of the Meister, but, after a period of intense reflection followed by revelation, reached the same conclusion that Mind is all. Eddy has been criticized for some of her theories and personal style, but one cannot find a flaw in the underlying foundation of her Christian Science when it is compared with the inner teachings of the world's great religions. One may have to dig for these gems in her prodigious output, but it is there, and in sync with both Eckhart and the *Gita* in its core Self realization. "...there are not two bases of being, matter and mind, but one alone,—Mind." Mary Baker Eddy, *Science and Health*, (The Mary Baker Eddy Foundation, 1910; reprint, 1986), 279. And again: "...Mind is *one*, including noumenon and phenomena, God and His thoughts. Mortal mind is a solecism in language, and involves an improper use of the word *mind*. As Mind is immortal, the phrase mortal mind implies something untrue and therefore unreal; and as the phrase is used in teaching Christian Science, it is meant to designate that which has no real existence." Ibid., 114.
5. Eckhart, Sermon 29, *Sermons*, 1:215.
6. Swami Satprakashananda, *Methods of Knowledge According to Advaita Vedanta*, (Calcutta: Advaita Asharama, 1974), 89.
7. Ibid.

which will resonate throughout the *Gita* and which mirrors a recurring motif in the Meister's sermons. That theme is the need for *detachment*.

"Grow attached, and you become addicted,"[8] says Krishna. "The uncontrolled mind does not guess that the *Atman* (the Self as experienced in—or as—the individual soul) is present.[9] When a man can still the senses, I call him illumined. The recollected mind is awake in the knowledge of the Atman."[10]

For Meister Eckhart, detachment as a precondition to knowledge is so important that he has several different words and phrases to describe its various forms, including: passive letting go or *Gelassenheit*; active renunciation or *Abgescheidenheit*; and poverty of spirit.[11] We cannot hope to understand our true nature, which is one with God's nature,[12] unless we first detach ourselves not only from the world of senses, but also from the snare of dualism, of viewing the world, God and ourselves as somehow fragmented and inharmonious. In opposition to the prevailing Christian attitude of his day, Eckhart goes a step further. Even outward austerities and renunciation can be a form of attachment as dangerous as any sin or frivolity. "...if a man thinks he can get God by (spiritual practices), it's like taking God, wrapping a cloak around his head and shoving Him under a bench! For whoever seeks God in a special way gets the way and misses God, who lies hidden in it."[13]

---

8. *Gita*, trans. Prabhavananda-Isherwood, 2:62.

9. Ibid., 2:66.

10. Ibid., 2:68-71. While I prefer it for readability, the Prabhavananda-Isherwood translation does not number the verses, and sometimes the translation is a free expression of a sentiment contained in several verses. Where I use verse numbers in quoting from this translation, I have cross-referenced the citation against the Aurobindo, Nikhilananda and Besant translations, which contain verse numbers.

11. This is the subject of Eckhart, Sermon 87, *Sermons*, 1:52. McGinn (135-6) states that Edmund Colledge and others found that this sermon's treatment of poverty of spirit echoes Marguerite Porete's *The Mirror of Simple Souls*; however, not to suggest that Eckhart copied from Porete, because spiritual poverty interested him long before Porete published her book in 1306.

12. But not the *same* as God's nature. "God is in the soul...but he is not the soul," Eckhart, Sermon 56, *Sermons*, 1:81. The individual soul in Eckhart is a small slice of an infinitely large pie.

13. Eckhart, Sermon 13b, *Sermons*, 1:117-8.

The penitent can become attached to his penance, the saint to her good works, reinforcing the dualistic chasm separating ideal God from imperfect humanity. "...some people do not understand this well," preached Eckhart in one of his vernacular sermons. "They are those who are attached to their own penances and external exercises, which seem important to people. God help those who hold divine truth in such low esteem! Such people present an outward picture that gives them the name of saints; but inside they are donkeys, for they cannot distinguish divine truth."[14]

In describing the path of knowledge, Krishna urges Arjuna to overcome the three tendencies that bind us to the illusion that the world is divided. These tendencies (gunas), discussed in detail in Chapter XIV, are sattwa (the spiritual), rajas (the passionate), and tamas (the ignorant). Eckhart is clearly in the spirit of the Gita when he rejects even spiritual practices as a sure-fire path to divine knowledge. "You, Arjuna, must overcome the three gunas," says Krishna. "You must be free from the pairs of opposites. Poise your mind in tranquility. Take care neither to acquire nor to hoard. Be established in the consciousness of Atman, always."[15] It is important to note that in neither the works of Eckhart nor in the Gita is detachment viewed as a form of punishment, deprivation, or discomfort. A wine lover would not spoil her enjoyment of a rare Bordeaux by drinking it with spicy food in a crowded, brightly lit room filled with noisy people and loud music. Even for something so mundane, a connoisseur would demand circumstances conducive to undivided attention and maximum pleasure. How much more does the seeker after God desire to be detached from distractions (and he or she can learn to do this even in the midst of confusion and daily responsibilities by following the path recommended by both of our authors).

In both bodies of work, even monastic vows and the scriptures take second place when the goal is divine knowledge. Krishna says, "When the whole country is flooded, the reservoir becomes superfluous. So, to the illumined seer, the Vedas are all superfluous." Eckhart's words to monks about vows that

---

14. *Meister Eckhart: The Essential Sermons, Commentaries, Treatises, and Defense*, Edmund Colledge and Bernard McGinn (Mahwah: Paulist Press, 1981), 199. I quote from Sermon 52 in this edition (and DW), which corresponds to Sermon 87 in the Walshe translation.
15. *Gita*, 45.

inhibit their realization is "…give it up! For any work that brings you nearer to God and God's embrace is the best."[16]

How do we recognize the person who has attained this state of unified knowledge, Arjuna asks.[17] Krishna replies that this person can be identified as one who "knows bliss in the Atman and wants nothing else." Free from cravings, fear and anger, his quiet mind is established in peace. What others see as darkness, the enlightened one knows as light: "Brahman and he are one."[18] And in Eckhart: "God and I: we are one."[19]

16. Eckhart, Sermon 3, *Sermons,* 1:35.
17. Like the author of the *Gita,* Eckhart often interjects a questioner into his sermons, a kind of devil's advocate asking the tough questions that the Meister's critics would be quick to suggest.
18. *Gita,* 47-50.
19. Meister Eckhart, Sermon 65, *Sermon and Treatises, vol. 2,* trans. M.O'C. Walshe (Longmead, Shaftsbury: Element Books, 1987), 136. I cite Raymond B. Blakney's more mellifluous rendering, found as Sermon 18 in *Meister Eckhart,* trans. Raymond B. Blakney (New York: Harper Torchbooks, 1941), 182.

3

The Yoga of Work

In the popular imagination, yoga is the antithesis of work. It conjures up visions of idle *saddhus* sitting in a cross-legged position, twisted in impractical postures, or lying flat on their backs, contemplating their navels, supposedly thinking of the infinite. Books on yoga often may be found in the "Hobby" section of the bookshop where a browser may look for something that is not work-related. Yoga, it would seem, is something people do when they are not working.

In reality, nothing could be further from the truth. The Sanskrit word *yoga* actually refers to work, as in the yoke (the literal translation of *yoga)* that engages a person to the business of living. The word *karma* (the magnetism of the *results* of our activities which pulls us back into repeated rebirths) also means work or works. In fact, *karma yoga* (the yoga of work) is the process of harnessing this irresistible power for good and using work as a ladder in the ascent to knowledge of God.[1] This chapter of the *Gita* is devoted specifically to the yoga of work in all its definitions. In addition to putting the role of work in Hinduism into perspective, it also sheds light on Meister Eckhart's own ideas about how a person follows a spiritual path while remaining engaged in the everyday world.

At the beginning of the chapter, Arjuna expresses confusion over the concept of work as separate and distinct from spiritual contemplation and asks

---

1. Yoga acknowledges several major paths of ascent: *karma yoga* (the yoga of work or action), *bhakti yoga* (the yoga of love or devotion), *jnana yoga* (the yoga of knowledge), and *raja yoga* (the yoga of meditation).

Krishna to tell him one definite way to reach the Truth. Krishna replies that *in the world* (that is, the everyday way we experience life) there are in fact two paths to enlightenment suited to different spiritual types. For persons of a contemplative bent, there is the path of knowledge. For those inclined to deeds, there is the path of selfless action.[2] Because these lead to the same goal—union with the divine—in reality, they are the same, two halves of one experiential coin, although at this stage, Arjuna does not have enough understanding to grasp this subtle verity. Work (activity) is part of our nature, as it is of God.[3] Every being must act or work according to the law of our tendencies, to be oriented toward spirituality, action, or sloth (the three *gunas* referenced in Chapter II to be treated in greater detail in Chapter XIV of the *Gita*). A person can control the senses, which are channels for these tendencies, only through force of will and by practicing detachment and disinterest.

Where Krishna sees two paths in the world of work, Eckhart sees two spirits representing work and contemplation standing "over all things, yet under God, on the circle of eternity," as he describes it in Sermon 9 in the story of Martha and Mary.[4] As described in Luke 10, Jesus is visiting the house of two sisters, Martha and Mary. These sisters are as different as day and night. Martha, whom the Meister believes is much older, fusses about the house making preparations for the Lord's visit, while Mary, the dreamer, sits adoringly at the Master's feet drinking in wisdom. Martha's path is action, Mary's is contemplation. The Meister enjoys turning the tables, however, and in his interpretation, counter to most Christian readings, it is Martha who has the upper hand. When she tells Jesus to release Mary so she can do her chores, she is not the whiny do-gooder criticizing the dreamy but inactive idealist. Rather, she says these words with a gentle, knowing smile that she shares with Christ. "Poor Mary," she seems to say. "Oh Lord, don't let her stay low (literally and figuratively) at your feet where she will become hopelessly mired in admiration. That won't do a thing for her spiritual growth! Let her rise up and join me, an older, more experienced seeker, in fusing wisdom and contemplation with actions in the world of work." Jesus's words support Martha, in Eckhart's reading, when he says that Mary has chosen the best part. According to Eck-

---

2. *Gita*, 51.
3. *Gita*, 51-52.
4. Eckhart, Sermon 9, *Sermons*, 1:83.

hart, he means, "Never fear, Martha…this will pass. The best thing that can befall a creature shall be hers: *she shall be blessed like you.*"[5]

Eckhart's theory of work as a path to enlightenment clearly was based in part on his own experience. Reading his uplifting words about the union of God and the soul, it is easy to forget that the Meister was not an ivy-towered ascetic, but a person of action thoroughly engaged in the world around him. His tasks as the leading Dominican administrator in Saxony (half of the German nation), in the cities of Cologne, Strasburg, and Erfurt, kept him as busy and challenged as the CEO of any major corporation. His responsibilities as the Dominican chair in Paris involved heated, contentious debates and the need to ever "guard one's back" against adversaries. Over the years, he was the spiritual leader of more than fifty convents and *Beguine* communities, demanding a complete shift of consciousness to become open to women's sensibilities and the unique female theology emerging in the 13th and 14th centuries. Further, he was physically a hearty, robust man, required, as a Dominican, to walk hundreds of miles when traveling from city to city, a harsh lifestyle that tended to weed out the frail and vulnerable at an early age.

The richness of his experience flavors Eckhart's full-bodied discourse on work. In his discussion of Martha and Mary, the Meister mentioned the "circle of eternity," and goes on to explain what he means through the description of three pathways to the divine: action, contemplation, and direct apprehension. These paths take the seeker,

- Through conventional yearning and action. "…to seek God in all creatures with manifold activity and ardent longing" (example: King David, "In all things have I sought rest," Eccles. 24:7);

- Through openness and receptivity to divine guidance. "…a wayless way, free and yet bound, raised, rapt away well nigh past self and all things, without will and without images, even though not yet in essential being" (example: Christ, "You are blessed, Peter, flesh and blood have not illumined you, but being caught up in the higher mind. When you call me God, my heavenly Father has revealed it to you." Matt. 16:17);

---

5.   Ibid., 86.

• Through immediate, direct apprehension. This is not a way at all, but "really being at home...seeing God without means in his own being..." (example: Christ, "I am the way, the truth, and the life," John 14:6).[6]

In the *Talks of Instruction*, written perhaps 10 years earlier for an audience of Dominican novices, Eckhart explains that work of any type undertaken on any path is not for the undisciplined person:

> Above all things a man must see to it that he trains himself strictly and well. If an untrained, unpractised man wanted to conduct himself and behave like a trained man, he would destroy himself and nothing would ever come of him. Once a man has first quite weaned himself of all things and become a stranger to them, then he can faithfully perform all his tasks, and delight in them or leave them alone without hindrance. But whatever a man loves or takes pleasure in and willfully follows, whether it be food or drink or anything else, this cannot be maintained without harm in an untrained man. A man must train himself not to seek his own in anything, but to find and take God in all things. For God does not give, and has never given any gift which a man might take and rest content with it...There is no manner of standing still for us in this life, and never has been for any man, however advanced he might be. Above all things, a man must ever be directed towards God's gifts, and ever anew.[7]

Eckhart reminds us that our attention is as appropriately directed in the world as in our devotions if our heart is full of God: "It is true that one piece of work differs from another, but if a man were to do all things with an equal mind, then indeed his works would all be equal, and for a man in a right state, who should thus possess God, God would shine forth as nakedly in the most worldly things as in the most godly."[8] How perfectly we see this sentiment

---

6. Ibid., 83-84.
7. Meister Eckhart, *Talks of Instruction*: Instruction 21 in *Sermons*, 3:46-47
8. Ibid., 20

through the words of Krishna: "Let the wise…show by example how work is holy when the heart of the worker is fixed on the Highest."[9]

But both masters go one step further, moving from work to works. Emptying out our hearts of the small self and all its petty concerns, allowing the presence of God to fill up the resulting vacuum (or to express a Presence that was always there, unacknowledged), we no longer need to engage in penances, austerities, or showy "good works" designed to help us earn merit. "…when a man has found delight and satisfaction and peace in the Atman, then he is no longer obliged to perform any kind of action…Do your duty always, but without attachment. That is how a man reaches the ultimate truth," states Krishna.[10] "If someone knows himself to be well trained in true inwardness, then let him drop all outward disciplines, even those he is bound to,"[11] writes Eckhart in the same spirit, adding an element which is distinctly Christian in feeling: "…if you would capture and curb (your worldly nature and activity) in a thousand times better fashion, then put on the bridle of love!…God lies in wait for us with nothing so much as with love…the more you are caught, the more you are free."[12]

As Eckhart goes deeper into the Ground of the Soul, as revealed in his later writing and preaching, the word "love" appears less frequently, but only because the word itself no longer is large enough for the state of being it represents.

---

9.   *Gita*, 55.
10. Ibid., 54.
11. McGinn, quoting from his translation of Sermon 104 (Walshe's Sermon 4), 69.
12. Eckhart, Sermon 4, *Sermons*, 1:46.

4

Renunciation through Knowledge
(The Birth of the Word
in the Ground of the Soul)

In the fourth chapter of the *Gita*, Krishna speaks of his own nature, which is eternal. One way his incarnation is expressed is through a return to human form in the world when "goodness grows weak, when evil increases;" i.e., as an *avatar* to guide and perhaps to save humankind when it strays from the path to God. It is not as Krishna that God demands veneration, but as God. Krishna or any other avatar is simply an expression of God among us, a reminder in the flesh to heed the scriptures, to practice yoga, to seek the Atman.

This is a different view of incarnation than that offered by traditional Western Christianity, which typically suggests that God entered the world as flesh one time, for a period of thirty-three years, was mysteriously resurrected, and lives on in his followers through the gift of the Holy Spirit.[1] But Eckhart is not so traditional as he would like us (or would have liked his inquisitors) to believe. Time and again, throughout his later sermons and other works, such as the *Book of Divine Comfort*, Eckhart takes the birth of God in the world to another level where the Son (or Word) is born (or spoken), not once in Bethlehem, but eternally and at every moment in the Ground of the Soul. This is a

---

1.   Admittedly, this is a hopelessly inadequate description of diverse Christian beliefs.

difficult doctrine to explain, and Eckhart repeatedly admits the same, but has such love and regard for every soul, no matter how uneducated and simplistic, that he is compelled to preach this core message irrespective of the sophistication of his audience.[2]

A similar challenge faces Krishna as he reveals infinite truth to a finite person. Arjuna, like the Meister's lay audience, is not a subtle theologian. Does he really understand what Krishna is saying when the Lord states, "I *seem* to be born: it is only seeming, only my *Maya*."[3] The hypothetical brother who asks the Meister questions in Sermon 1 could just as well be Arjuna seeking literal answers from his Charioteer: "But sir, where is the silence and where is the place where the word is spoken?" And the Meister replies, "As I said just now, it is in the purest thing that the soul is capable of, in the noblest part, in the ground—indeed, in the very essence of the soul which is the soul's most secret part. There is the silent 'middle,' for no creature ever entered there and no image, nor has the soul there either activity or understanding, therefore she is not aware *there* of any image, whether of herself or of any other creature."[4]

Christologically speaking, Eckhart appears to have been out of step with other theologians of his age.[5] Rather than dwell on the flesh-and-blood Christ in all his suffering glory, Eckhart identifies each soul as the seat of the potentially manifested Son of God. Reading Eckhart's work, there are "no pictures of the infant Jesus in the crib or meditations on the bloody Christ on the cross. There is little consideration of the historical events of Christ's life. At times, Eckhart seems to go out of his way to avoid an obvious Christological reading of a text."[6]

No more vividly is Eckhart's original view of the incarnation expressed than in Sermon 71. At a time when heresy in all its forms was being vigorously

---

2.   This was a major charge against him during his heresy trial, that he misled the simple who were not prepared to understand complex theological arguments. Ironically, Eckhart is fully in the Patristic tradition in making such statements (Tertullian: "The soul is by nature Christian.")
3.   *Gita*, 60.
4.   Eckhart, Sermon 1, *Sermons*, 1:3. One is tempted to ask, however, if one is not aware of the birth of the Son taking place in the soul, does it in fact occur? Or does it take place whether we *recognize* it or not?
5.   McGinn, 115.
6.   McGinn, 115-6.

hounded and uprooted, what level of derring-do, arrogance, or supreme self-confidence in God's revelation led Eckhart to utter the following words:

> The soul in no way differs from our Lord Jesus Christ except in that the soul has a coarser essence: for his essence is in the eternal Person. But as far as she can lay aside her coarseness—if she could lay this aside altogether—she would be completely the same, and *whatever can be said of our Lord Jesus Christ, could be said fully of the soul.*[7]

And yet, viewing this and similar unorthodox descriptions of the Christian Savior through the lens of the *Gita*, Chapter IV, one is struck by a kind of euphony that resonates between distant cultures separated by a thousand years. Who is to say that the "birthless, deathless Lord of all that breathes"[8] is not indistinguishable from the incarnation born eternally in the essence of the soul? "Whatever path men travel is my path," says Krishna. "No matter where they walk it leads to me."[9]

Krishna uses this revelatory moment to emphasize his changeless nature, repeating a *Leitmotif* that recurs throughout the *Gita*: "I am beyond action." With this declaration, the Hindu Lord defines and distinguishes between action and inaction. The renunciation through knowledge that forms the theme of this chapter is not necessarily the renunciation commonly associated in the West with Hinduism. Krishna praises the renunciant who is able to turn his or her back on the world, but equally celebrates the follower who renounces the fruits of action while continuing to function fully in the world of *samsara*. This renunciant, full of the knowledge of what matters most, "...acts and is beyond action...acts and earns no evil...acts and is not bound by his action...If a man sees Brahman in every action, he will find Brahman."[10]

This renunciation is not punitive or a kind of "do it because I say so" order by the Supreme Being. Rather, it is an admonition to keep our "eye on the prize," which, in this case, is nothing short of total enlightenment, immersion

---

7. Eckhart, Sermon 71, Sermons, 2:183, my italics. I find myself wanting to shout out over the centuries to the Meister, "No, stop, don't say it! *Think* it, whisper it to your closest disciples, but don't *say* it!"
8. *Gita*, 60.
9. Ibid., 61.
10. Ibid., 63-64.

in the Godhead. By renouncing attachment to the results of action/activity/ work, the seeker demonstrates his or her allegiance to knowledge over ignorance. "When you have reached enlightenment, ignorance will delude you no longer. In the light of that knowledge, you will see the entire creation within your own Atman and in me."[11] In the next chapter of the *Gita*, we can see this more clearly in Meister Eckhart's teaching on the passive (*Gelassenheit*) and active (*Abgescheidenheit*) aspects of detachment.

---

11. Ibid., 66.

5

The Yoga of Renunciation

Two of the terms inextricably associated with Meister Eckhart's teaching are the words for *detachment*: *Gelassenheit* and *Abgescheidenheit*. And yet seldom have two words with similar definitions held such a different inner meaning. The person who would renounce the world to seek a better life must cultivate both forms in order to achieve his or her goal, the master taught.

In Chapter V of the *Gita*, Krishna observes that it is "hard to renounce action without following the yoga of action."[1] The person of action "puts aside desire, offering the act to Brahman...he rests on action, untouched by action."[2] This is *Abgescheidenheit*, the active form of renunciation, where, to use a Victorian phrase, one "fights manfully onward"[3] to aggressively fight the unruly senses, much as St. Anthony fought the desert demons.

> Shutting off the sense
> From what is outward,
> Fixing the gaze
> At the root of the eyebrows,
> Checking the breath-stream

---

1. Ibid., 70
2. Ibid., 71
3. A line from a Protestant hymn of the muscular Christianity type: "Fight manfully onward/Dark shadows subdue/Look ever to Jesus,/He'll carry you through." The hymn was written by Horatio R. Palmer, according to information at the Web site, http://www.gospelcom.net/chi/ARCHIVEF/04/daily-04-26-2001.shtml.

> In and outgoing
> Within the nostrils,
> Holding the senses,
> Holding the intellect,
> Holding the mind fast,
> He who seeks freedom,
> Thrusts fear aside,
> Thrusts aside anger
> And puts off desire:
> Truly that man
> Is made free forever.[4]

In the *Talks of Instruction*, written to encourage beginning monastics, the Meister also admonishes seekers to exert themselves in overcoming the world's hypnotizing attractions. "…learn to be unattached in your works…" he exhorts. "Skillful diligence is required for this, and in particular two things. One is that a man has shut himself off well inwardly, so that his mind is on its guard against the images without, that they remain without and do not unfittingly keep company and walk with him, and that they find no resting-place in him. The second is that he should not let himself become caught up by his internal imagery, whether it be in the form of pictures or lofty thoughts, or outward impressions or whatever is present to his mind, or be distracted, nor dissipate himself in their multiplicity."[5]

Eckhart, as is his wont, goes a step further in the treatise, *On Detachment*, straining against the boundaries that define Christian doctrine. In the face of Christ's declaration that the greatest commandments are "to love God and persons" and quoting Paul's famous admonition to love in I Corinthians 13, Eckhart nonetheless asserts that "I extol detachment above any

---

4.   Ibid., 77.
5.   Eckhart, *Sermons, The Talks of Instruction,* 3:45. Here the Meister reflects the thought of another Yoga master he would not have read or heard about: Patanjali. In his seminal *Yoga Sutras*, Patanjali cautions the student of Yoga not to be distracted by visions which will do more harm than good in the systematic journey into the Godhead.

love."[6] Eckhart's justification is fascinating and reminds one of nothing so much as the principle of displacement and conservation of energy in physics.[7]

First, because, at best, love constrains me to love God, but detachment compels God to love me. Now it is a far nobler thing my constraining God to me than for me to constrain myself to God. That is because God is more readily able to adapt Himself to me, and can more easily unite with me than I could unite with God. That detachment *forces God to me*, I can prove thus: everything wants to be in its natural place. Now God's natural place is unity and purity, and that comes from detachment. Therefore God is bound to give Himself to a detached heart.[8]

A second element, the Meister points out, is that detachment "makes me receptive to nothing but God." So, in effect, one could say that love is still the greatest commandment, but the way to experience that love is through a detachment that causes God to rush in irresistibly and fill up the vacuum caused by renunciation of everything else. "Now detachment is so nearly nothing," says Eckhart, "that there is no thing subtle enough to maintain itself in detachment except God alone. He is so subtle and so simple that He can stay in a detached heart. Therefore detachment is receptive of nothing but God."[9]

There is a fine but significant line dividing the "self control" that Krishna advocates and the "self denial" Eckhart calls for. "Self controlled, cut free from desire, curbing the heart, and knowing the Atman, man finds Nirvana that is in Brahman, here and hereafter,"[10] the Hindu Lord states in this chapter, describing a state of renunciation undertaken to achieve specific goals that the individual seeker desires (e.g., eternal enjoyment of God, the pleasurable state

---

6. Ibid., *On Detachment*, 117.
7. Or the reciprocity and interdependence of yin and yang in Taoism.
8. Ibid., 118.
9. Ibid. Eckhart's "negative theology" is sometimes misconstrued to suggest at kind of agnosticism. These lines suggest the contrary: that God Himself is not "nothing," though He may be "no thing," but rather by letting go of "all things" and embracing "nothingness," we create the space in which God makes Himself manifest as the great All within our hearts.
10. *Gita*, 76.

of Nirvana, etc.). Eckhart's self denial differs sharply, for even the desires of the seeker must be abandoned to let God rush in with his irrepressible love:

> Now our Lord says, "Whoever abandons anything for me and for my name's sake, I will return it to him a hundredfold, with eternal life to boot" (Matt. 19:29). But if you give it up for the sake of that hundredfold and for eternal life, you have given up nothing, even if you give it up for a thousandfold reward you are giving up nothing. *You must give up yourself*, altogether give up self, and then you have really given up."[11]

For the Meister, attachment to future bliss, as surely as clinging to austerities and deprivations themselves (a popular obsession among the medieval religious), steers the seeker into a spiritual *cul de sac*. Self denial is not mortification but rather surrender, letting go of anything that gets in God's way, most notably ourselves, our false sense of self. With the ebbing of "mine" comes the fullness of "Thine." This kind of renunciation is no actual deprivation for the individual, but rather a complete fulfillment in the part of the soul—its very ground—that is eternal and uncreated. In Sermon 17, Eckhart states with the force of revelation that there is "something that transcends the created being of the soul,"[12] and ticks off these characteristics as:

• Akin to the nature of deity;

• One in itself;

• Having naught in common with anything;

• A strange and desert place;

• Rather nameless than possessed of a name;

• More unknown than it is known.

---

11. Eckhart, Sermon 17, *Sermons*, 1:142.
12. Ibid, 144.

And yet, "as long as you mind yourself or any thing at all, you know no more of God than my mouth knows of colour or my eye of taste: so little do you know or discern what God is."[13]

Krishna describes for Arjuna, who represents the active person, the active path of renunciation leading to this immersion in what matters most. While the Meister invites the seeker to "let go and let God" (to use a 20th century phrase from Alcoholics Anonymous), Krishna offers concrete suggestions to an individual trained in the military disciplines: turn off your senses through yoga, fix your sight at the *chakra* between the eyebrows, observe *pranayama* (carefully controlled yogic breathing), control the *vritti*, the oscillating currents of the mind. These disciplines will lead to the highest knowledge and the fulfillment of one's true nature.

> When thus he knows me
> The end, the author
> Of every offering
> And all austerity,
> Lord of the worlds
> And the friend of all men:
> O son of Kunti
> Shall he not enter
> The peace of my presence?[14]

---

13. Ibid.
14. *Gita,.* 77.

6

The Yoga of Meditation

In his discourse on renunciation, Krishna touched on several of the practices which form the first part of what is known as the eight limbs of yoga. The eight limbs were codified in Patanjali's *Yoga Sutras*, the seminal work on yoga practice developed (probably by several authors) some time between the 4th century B.C.E. and the 4th century C.E. Designed to lead the seeker scientifically to God-realization, the eight-fold path of yoga consists of the following steps:

1. *yama*, moral conduct,

2. *niyama*, religious observances,

3. *asana*, correct posture,

4. *pranayama*, control of *prana*, subtle life currents, by means of breathing techniques,

5. *pratyahara*, withdrawal of the mind from sense objects,

6. *dharana*, holding the mind to one thought,

7. *dhyana*, meditation,

8. *samadhi*, superconsciousness, union with the divine[1].

---

1. *Autobiography of a Yogi*, Paramahansa Yogananda, (Los Angeles: Self-Realization Fellowship, 1979), pp. 262-263; and *Threads of Yoga: The Yoga Sutras of Patanjali*, Linda Holt, California State University-Dominguez Hills, 1993. Yogananda clearly explains in his book how the eight limbs of Yoga differs from the Eightfold Path of Buddhism. The Yoga path is progressive and sequential, whereas the eight venues of the Buddhist path are concurrent.   **50**

These progressive steps enable the active person to remain in the world and yet develop the kind of detachment that leads to spiritual fulfillment. In Chapter VI, Krishna moves on to describe the higher stages of *raja* or royal yoga in which the illusion that God and human are two, not one, dissolves and melts away.

Krishna opens this discourse by stating that the person who is disinterested in the fruits of his action has achieved a higher level of attainment than some-one who follows all the rules of yoga but is still attached to their accomplishments. "…when he nears that height of oneness, his acts will fall from him, his path will be tranquil."[2]

It is worth noting that as the seeker progresses along the spiritual path, self-discipline and force of will have less to do with advancement toward union. Assertion and self-control are essential for getting started at the early stages of service and physical mastery, but once these are attained, the language Krishna uses is more receptive than aggressive: "his acts…fall from him," which suggests something similar to Meister Eckhart's *Gelassenheit*.

Between 1295 and 1298, when he was not yet an acknowledged Master (though serving as Vicar of Thuringia and Prior of Erfurt), Eckhart delivered a series of informal talks to Dominican novices in question and answer format not dissimilar to the dialogue between Krishna and Arjuna. Although these talks (which we know as the *Talks of Instruction*) do not contain the dramatic revelations, bracing humor, or shocking language of Eckhart's later, possibly "post-realization" sermons, they offer a fitting counterpart to the *Gita*'s instructions to *sannyasins* (as we saw in Chapter V and will continue to note in Chapter VI).

Having described the importance of exerting the will to control the senses and not succumbing to intriguing mental imagery or visions, Eckhart moves ahead (in Yoga-like progression) to recommend stilling and focusing the mind (*dharana* and *dhyana* in Yoga). Consider what he has to say about prayer, sometimes one of the noisiest of supposedly "quiet" Christian practices:

> The most powerful prayer, one well-nigh omnipotent to gain all things, and the noblest work of all is that which proceeds from a bare mind. The more bare it is, the more powerful, worthy, useful, praiseworthy and perfect the prayer and the work. A bare mind can

2.   *Gita*, 79.

do all things. What is a bare mind? A bare mind is one which is worried by nothing and is tied to nothing, which has not bound its best part to any mode, does not seek its own in anything, that is fully immersed in God's dearest will and gone out of its own. A man can do no work however paltry that does not derive power and strength from this source. We should pray so intently, as if we would have all members and all powers turned to it—eyes, ears, mouth, heart and all the senses; and we should never stop until we find ourselves about to be united with Him whom we have in mind and are praying to: that is—God.[3]

In a similar vein, Krishna notes, "If a yogi has perfect control over his mind, and struggles continually in this way to unite himself with Brahman, he will come at last to the crowning peace of Nirvana, the peace that is in me."[4] In making the leap, however, from the active individual to the person immersed in Brahman, the *Gita* describes a step that the Meister never takes, although the history of the Christian tradition is full of hermits, recluses, and solitary holy people who have taken this step of *solitary contemplation*:

The yogi should retire into a solitary place, and live alone. He must exercise control over his mind and body. He must free himself from the hopes and possessions of this world. He should meditate on the Atman unceasingly.

The place where he sits should be firm, neither too high nor too low, and situated on a clean spot. He should first cover it with sacred grass, then with a deer skin; then lay a cloth over these. As he sits there, he is to hold the senses and imagination in check, and keep the mind concentrated upon its object. If he practices meditation in this manner, his heart will become pure.[5]

---

3.   Eckhart, "Of the Most Powerful Prayer and the Highest Activity" in *Talks of Instruction, Sermons*, 3:12-13.
4.   *Gita*, 82.
5.   Ibid, 81.

Compare this with the Meister's remarks to young monks, the yogis of the medieval Rhineland:

> I was asked: "Some people shun all company and always want to be alone, their peace depends on it, and on being in church. Was that the best thing?" And I said, "No!" Now if man is in a right state, in truth he has God with him. Now, if a man truly has God with him, God is with him everywhere, in the street or among people just as much as in church or in the desert or in a cell. If he possesses God truly and solely, such a man cannot be disturbed by anybody.[6]

And yet, ten years or so later, the Meister does concede in a more intimate, less didactic sermon, that yogic stillness—in search of which a seeker may want to withdraw from the world of the senses, at least for a time—is a necessity in order to cultivate the barrenness, the desert, the bare mind in which God will reveal Himself inexorably. In Sermon 10, a hypothetical monk asks, "Isn't it better to 'do something' like pray or do good deeds to dispel the gloom and monotony of emptiness?" "No, be sure of this," says the Meister. "Absolute stillness for as long as possible is best of all for you. You cannot exchange this state for any other without harm."[7] Eckhart goes so far as to suggest that all outward disciples, *even those a monk or nun has vowed to follow*, must be dropped in order to experience "true inwardness."[8]

Krishna's words to Arjuna enlarge on this idea: "Patiently, little by little, a man must free himself from all mental distractions, with the aid of the intelligent will. He must fix his mind upon the Atman, and never think of anything else. No matter where the restless and unquiet mind wanders, it must be drawn back and made to submit to the Atman only."[9] To reach the highest form of communion with the divine, even sacraments and sacramentals, ritu-

---

6.   Eckhart, "On Detachment and on Possessing God," in *Talks of Instruction, Sermons*, 3:16.
7.   Eckhart, Sermon 10, *Sermons*, 1:43.
8.   Ibid., 46. This is elaborated on in McGinn, 69.
9.   *Gita*, 83.

als, rites, even good works must for the time fall aside, to create the space for God to rush in and fulfill the life of the individual devotee.

> Utterly quiet,
> Made clean of passion,
> The mind of the yogi
> Knows that Brahman,
> His bliss is the highest...
>
> The way is easy,
> Brahman has touched him,
> That bliss is boundless.[10]

According to McGinn, Eckhart believes that when God enters or reveals Himself in the soul, He replaces the active intellect.[11] When the active mind has been subsumed in the Godhead, then it matters not whether there are images, deeds, or activities, for it is God (the Self, or our true nature, in Yoga) that is the mover, not the individual (or self with a lower-case "s").[12] In the four sermons which form what is known as "the Christmas cycle"[13] the Meister explains what he means by this signature concept of absolute emptiness and stillness as a prerequisite for the birth of the Son (or Word) in the Ground of the Soul, or, as we may interpret this, the experience of deep meditation which leads to the unity of self and Self. In Sermon 3, Eckhart differentiates between the active intellect which "abstracts images from outward things, stripping them of matter..." and the passive intellect into which these filtered, matter-free images are channeled.[14] When the active intellect is silent and

---

10. Ibid, 84.
11. McGinn, *Mystical Theology*, 68.
12. This is the author's inference and interpretation, not McGinn's.
13. Walshe, Sermons I through IV. Walshe's numbering system follows Pfeiffer and is not intended to place the sermons in chronological order. These sermons are obviously very mature works and suggest that they were composed *after* Eckhart had experienced a deep devotional encounter. We may surmise from references and levels of maturity in his writing that Eckhart had this experience in his 40s. It is worth noting that many other mystics experienced mature revelations in early middle age, most notably (though more demonstrably) Hildegard of Bingen (1098-1179).
14. Eckhart, Sermon 3, *Sermons*, 1:29.

still, God cannot help but move in and displace the active intellect completely. This is a portrait of the meditation experience clear and simple: emptying the mind of self to allow the natural state of Being—the Almighty Itself—to be made manifest within.

As the Meister will preach a thousand years later, the *Gita* points to *panentheism*—the presence of God in all beings—as the ultimate state of reality. "That (enlightened) yogi sees me in all things, all things within me...He is established in union with me, and worships me devoutly in all beings," states Krishna.[15] Eckhart reaches a similar conclusion (echoing the pre-Socratic Heraclitus) when he preaches in Sermon 67, "A man who knew nothing but creatures would never need to attend to any sermons, for every creature is full of God and is a book."[16]

Awestruck by the magnitude of what Krishna suggests, Arjuna protests that the mind is so restless, wilder than any wind, how could anyone hope to tame it and experience this union? Krishna offers a practical step that Eckhart's listeners could as surely follow and with as excellent a result: practice, and exercise dispassion. "...a self-controlled man can master it, if he struggles hard, and uses the right means."[17] Just what these right means are is revealed in the chapters of the *Gita* which follow. The first is at once an expansion and a focus on the earlier discourse on knowledge. This time, it is knowledge refined, empowered, and sweetened by experience.

---

15. *Gita*, 84.
16. Eckhart, Sermon 67, *Sermons*, 2: 155.
17. Ibid., 86.

7

The Yoga of Knowledge and Experience

Few commonalities existed between the cultures of 2nd century B.C.E. Hindu India and the 14th century Christian Rhineland. And yet, there is one point on which surely the author of the *Gita* and Meister Eckhart would have agreed. The world of matter, everyday intelligence, and the senses is not the "real" world, the locus of what matters most. In Chapter VII, Krishna describes the eight manifestations of the phenomenal world as: earth, water, fire, air, ether, mind, intellect, and ego. The educated people of Meister Eckhart's time followed the teachings of Empedocles (c. 493-c. 433 B.C.E.) that the world ultimately, exclusively, and eternally was composed of four elements: earth, air, fire, and water.[1] For most medieval thinkers, soul and mind were related but different. For the Vedic sages of India, mind, intellect, and ego were simply more rarefied forms of the same "world stuff." Krishna reveals to Arjuna that behind this illusory world lurks the fundamental principle of consciousness inherent in all beings, that which infuses them with life and withdraws the life force in inevitable death. In sweeping language, the Lord attempts to describe

---

1. *The Longman Anthology of British Literature. Vol. 1.* New York: Addison Wesley Longman, Inc., 1999.

the imaginable power, grandeur, and majesty of this divine reservoir from which all phenomena derive their being:

> ...I am the birth of all cosmos:
> Its dissolution also.

> I am he who causes:
> No other beside me.
> Upon me, these worlds are held
> Like pearls strung on a thread.

> I am the essence of the waters,
> The shining of the sun and the moon:
> OM in all the Vedas,
> The word that is God.
> It is I who resound in the ether
> And am potent in man.[2]

Eckhart's view of God is equally grand, but less sensuously expressed.

All creatures God ever created or might yet create, if He wished, are little or nothing compared with God. Heaven is so vast and so wide that if I told you, you would not believe it. If you were to take a needle and prick the heavens with it, then that part of heaven that the needle-point pricked would be greater in comparison to heaven and the whole world, than heaven and the world are compared with God.[3]

What is added, however, to the description of the Elysian realm is once again the distinctly Christian element of love. In *bhakti* Yoga, the Yoga of love which is the subject of Chapter XII, the accent is on worshipful devotion rather than on the intimate love of God and humanity given by Jesus as the two great commandments.[4] "Know then," says the Meister, "that God loves

---

2. *Gita*, 89.
3. Eckhart, Sermon 42, *Sermons*, 1:293-4. Similar language is used in Sermon 73, *Sermons*, 2:194.
4. Of course, one cannot *command* anyone to love; perhaps what is meant is to become intentional and *open* to love, and to act in a loving manner, which will cause the gift of love to follow.

the soul so mightily, it is a wonder." Such a wonder, in fact, that Eckhart provides a rather startling metaphor: "If anyone were to rob God of loving the
soul, he would rob Him of His life and being, *or he would kill God*, if one may
say so; for the self-same love with which God loves the soul is His life, and in
that same love the Holy Ghost blossoms forth, and that same love *is* the Holy
Ghost."[5] For Eckhart, love and detachment are not mutually exclusive. Eckhart's detachment, whether *Gelassenheit* or *Abgescheidenheit*, is not the cold
dark matter (to use a contemporary astronomical term) of masochistic repres-
sion and emotional strangulation, but rather a stilling of extraneous currents
(like the *vritti* or currents of the mind of classical Yoga) to allow the most sublime pleasure to move in and take over: the ecstasy of Divine Love romancing
and reclaiming its own Soul.

   This idea of a "loving detachment" is not unique to Eckhart, nor to Western mysticism. Krishna, too, distances divinity from the busy-ness of everyday
life. Everything that proceeds from the three *gunas*—the slothful *tamas*, the
hyperactive *rajas*, and the spiritual *sattwa*, all examined in greater detail in
Chapter XIV—proceeds from God, and is contained in Him, "but I am not in
them." The moods and mental imbalances that are caused by these swirling
forces that inform every aspect of phenomenal life keep humanity from recognizing the God among them…in fact, the God they are. "I stand apart from
them all (the *gunas*), supreme and deathless."[6] It is only by "taking refuge in
me" that the seeker can pass beyond *maya* (also known as *Prakriti*). Or, as
Eckhart would say, it is only when God rushes into the still, quiet, clarified
Ground of the Soul that illusion vanishes and truth is revealed.

   Both the *Gita* and Eckhart's vernacular teachings recognize that even in the
world of appearances, all is not black and white. As there are degrees of subtlety in material and spiritual states, so there are different kinds of seekers after
truth. Krishna names four types:

1. the world-weary

2. the seeker for knowledge

3. the seeker for happiness

---

5. Ibid., 294.
6. *Gita*, 90.

4. the person of spiritual discrimination (which, not surprisingly, is the most evolved type).[7]

Krishna tells Arjuna that all varieties of devotee are good, but none better than number four:

> ...the man of discrimination
> I see as my very Self.
> For he alone loves me
> Because I am myself:
> The last and only goal
> Of his devoted heart.[8]

In contrast, people with limited understanding pray only for what is temporal and subject to dissolution. Krishna says something very interesting at this point which echoes throughout the later work of the Dominican master: rites and rituals are not the most effective pathway to God. Blunted by "worldly desires," these individuals of limited understanding establish "this or that ritual or cult and resort to various deities, according to the impulse of their inborn natures."[9] Then the Hindu Lord makes a statement which, out of context, could be the Meister's very words: "...it does not matter what deity a devotee chooses to worship."

The lens of the *Gita* helps us focus on the words of Eckhart in Sermon 13b, his famous discourse on human nature:

> (If)...whenever what you do is done for the sake of the Kingdom of God, or for God's sake, or for eternal blessing, and thus really for ulterior motives, *you are wrong*. You may pass for a good person, but this is not the best. For truly, if you imagine that you are going to get more out of God by means of religious offices and devotions, in sweet retreats and solitary orisons, than you might by the fireplace or in the stable, then you might just as well think you could seize God and wrap a mantle around his head and stick him under the table! *To*

---

7. Ibid., 91.
8. Ibid., 92.
9. Ibid.

seek God by rituals is to get the ritual and lose God in the process, for he hides behind it.[10]

The path of renunciation that leads to this knowledge is further explored in Chapter VIII of the *Gita*, and is explicated, in ways both similar and dissimilar, in the Meister's vernacular work.

10. While this section is found in Sermon 13b Walshe, I have chosen to quote from Raymond B. Blakney's much-maligned, but occasionally incomparable translation. This passage may be found as Sermon 5 in Raymond Blakney, *Meister Eckhart*, (Harper & Row: New York, 1941), 127.

8

The Way to Eternal Brahman

One of the most remarkable qualities of Meister Eckhart's *oeuvre* is its utter lack of interest in death. Death was a leading theme among the clergy, artists, and scholars in the Middle Ages, who together described in excruciating detail the torments that awaited those who eschewed the seven cardinal virtues and pursued the seven deadly sins. Eckhart's sunny disposition, sense of humor, and conviction that all who aspire may attain the bliss of God in this very life run counter to his reputation as a "negative theologian," a distinction he shares with his contemporaries: the author of *The Cloud of Unknowing* and the radiant English mystic, Richard Rolle. The term, "negative theology," is, of course, misleading. When Eckhart states time and again that God is *nothing*, he is offering a point of view shared for millennia by the followers of Yoga and Vedanta. It would be more instructive, perhaps, to extend the metaphor to say, "God is nothing...that we can know through our reason or senses. He is no-thing, but rather the source of all being, the background against which the drama of phenomenal life unfolds."

Yet, the man who died six years before the arrival of the Black Death had no desire to terrify novitiates, nuns, monks, or the general public into a fearful Christianity whose only advantage was that it offered some hope of escape from the ravages of hell. James M. Clark reflects the observation of other Eckhart scholars when he writes that the Meister's references to hell are "few and perfunctory."[1] Rather than recite the grim fate that awaits the sinner, Meister Eckhart's work speaks of a positive, joyful life in God:

---

1. James M. Clark, *Meister Eckhart* (London: 1957), 53.

Now listen to a marvel! How marvelous to be without and within, to embrace and be embraced, to see and be the seen, to hold and be held—*that* is the goal, where the spirit is ever at rest, united in joyous eternity![2]

Krishna in Chapter VIII of the *Gita* speaks of two paths open to the person physically leaving his or her body: the path that leads to rebirth and the path of no return.[3] To Eckhart, it is not a matter of waiting until death, and at any rate, there is only one path[4] worth taking (and taking now, not later): the path of emptying the self, saying yes to God, and being open to the realization of divine bliss. Krishna describes the traditional Hindu doctrine of reincarnation, which holds that a soul will be reborn into the world time and again until he or she "gets it right," i.e., achieves the path to unitive consciousness, and, through the path of no return, merges with the Godhead at the moment of death (if not before, as is the case with some renunciants).

The Meister was probably not *directly* familiar with the Indian doctrine of reincarnation, though a good deal of Vedantic thought infiltrated the world of the medieval scholastics through the works of pre-Socratics such as Heraclitus, through Plato, Plotinus, and Proclus, and then through the Greek-influenced church fathers and mothers of the first 600 years C.E., such as Origen and the pseudo-Dionysius.[5] To judge by the extent to which the Meister references Proclus, Origen, and other masters from antiquity in his vernacular

2. Eckhart, Sermon 9, *Sermons*, 1:84-85.
3. *Gita*, 98.
4. Not to be confused with the *three pathways* described in Chapter III of this study, which are in fact three steps along the same single path.
5. Timothy J. Lomperis in *Hindu Influences on Greek Philosophy* claims as his central thesis that "…Plato, through the Pythagoreans and also the Orphics, was subjected to the influence of Hindu thought, but that he may not have been aware of it as coming from India." (76) Lomperis concedes, however, that coincidence also may account for similarities between Plato's work and the philosophies of India. Evidence exists that there was contact between Greek and Indian cultures at least in the early years of Christianity. Philostratus (ca. 220 C.E.) in *The Life of Appollonius of Tyana* states that the first century Greek sage visited Persia and India "where he consorted with the Brahmans," according to translator F.C. Conybeare (1856-1924). The translation is on-line at www.magna.com.au/~prfbrown/atyana00.html.

sermons, it is evident that they had a profound influence on his thought as well as his spiritual practice. And while reincarnation has never been part of mainstream Christianity, there is latitude in the interpretation of Greek scriptures for those who find the notion of rebirth compelling. The words of Jesus, "You must be born again," have long tantalized thinkers who may have wondered if Elijah had returned as John the Baptist or Jesus, or whether Christ was in fact speaking of reincarnation, a concept which would not have been in the frame of reference of his contemporaries and those who, years later, wrote down the words he may have said.

Be that as it may, Eckhart did not embrace the kind of reincarnation Krishna describes. Rebirth, however, as we have seen, *was* a major concern of the Dominican, who preached the eternal birth of the Son (Word) in the Ground of the Soul with enthusiasm and conviction. The seeker who experiences this birth in effect becomes reborn in this very life and becomes part of the ever-dynamic process that is God. This dynamism is experienced as the kind of ebb and flow (a key Eckhartian concept) that reminds us today of the processes of high-energy-particle physics or deep-space astronomy which describes unimaginably colossal galaxies flowing into and out of being.[6] McGinn suggests that a study of this flow is a "good way to understand Eckhart's implied systematics," noting the reciprocity of the "flowing-forth" of things from the hidden ground of God, and "flowing-back" (or "breaking through") of the universe into essential identity with this divine source."[7]

While Hindu reincarnation *per se* is foreign to the Meister, the metaphysics of flow is second nature to Krishna, who finds beyond the flowing-forth and flowing-back (like the plus and minus poles of electrical current) the ever-present One.

But behind the manifest and the unmanifest, there is another Existence, which is eternal and changeless. This is not dissolved in the

---

6. See Dennis Overbye's article, "In Dark Matter, New Hints of a Universal Glue," *The New York Times*, January 8, 2002. This article contains vivid descriptions that may serve as a metaphor for the processes of mystical union, such as the image of gravitational pull in space tugging "galaxies to and fro violently, distorting the orderly expansion of the universe," and, earlier, asking the question, "What if all this is just an illusion?"

7. McGinn, 71.

general cosmic dissolution. It has been called the unmanifest, the imperishable...Those who reach It are not reborn.[8]

Krishna tells Arjuna of the union beyond flow, where even the seemingly inescapable gravitational force of reincarnation stops dead. And so, in the context of his own set of traditions and cultural understandings, Eckhart also speaks of this union.

> Some simple folk imagine they will see God as if He were standing there and they here," he taught. "That is not so. God and I are one. Through knowledge I take God into myself (Ed.: flowing-forth), through love I enter into God (Ed.: flowing-back)...The work and the coming to be are one. If the carpenter does not work, the house does not come into existence. When the axe rests, the process stops. God and I are one in this operation: He works, and I come into being...Thus we are changed into God that we may know Him as He is...[9]

In a similar spirit, Krishna invites Arjuna to join him outside of the oscillating world of opposites and to follow the yoga that reaches deeper than the senses and farther than the stars: The Yoga of Mysticism.

---

8. *Gita*, 98.
9. Eckhart, Sermon 65, Sermons, 2:136-7.

9

The Yoga of Mysticism

"Do this (the Yoga of mysticism) and be free forever," Krishna tells Arjuna in Chapter IX of the *Gita*. "This is the knowledge above all other...only made plain to the eye of the mystic."[1] But what exactly is mysticism, can it be taught, and how, if at all, does this shed light on the teachings of Meister Eckhart?

Mysticism has been regarded as many things throughout history. Is it the stock in trade of the local Tarot card and palm reader? Or is it the sublime realm suggested by Plato's metaphor of the cave? We can dismiss popular mysticism, with its associations with fortune telling and entertainment, for purposes of this discussion. Evelyn Underhill, the 20th century English scholar of mysticism, provides a good general definition that can serve as a guide in interpreting both the *Gita* and Meister Eckhart:

> Mysticism is the art of union with Reality. The mystic is a person who has attained that union in greater or less degree; or who aims at and believes in that attainment.[2]

Krishna defines this Reality as Brahman: the ultimate source of all Being. For Eckhart, Reality is something beyond God: the absolute Godhead (*gotheit*), unknowable in the sense that it is both infinite and eternal; and the brain,

---

1. *Gita*, 100-101.
2. Evelyn Underhill, *Practical Mysticism* (E.P. Dutton: New York, 1915; reprint, Mineola, N.Y.: Dover Publications, 2000), 2.

our feeble instrument of knowing, is both finite and temporal. However, our *mind* or *soul* (and I believe Eckhart uses these terms more or less interchangeably) at some point intersects with the divine and knows the Godhead as certainly as it knows itself, for they are one. The spiritual seeker (who is a mystic to the degree that he or she seeks union) also steps outside the boundaries of time and place at the point where the Other becomes the Self. As Eckhart states it, the soul is eternally young:

> See! My soul is as young as the day it was created, yes, and much younger. I tell you, I should be ashamed if it were not younger tomorrow than it is today.[3]

More interesting from the *Gita's* perspective is Eckhart's declaration that the difference between God and Godhead is the difference between action and inaction:

> Everything that is in the Godhead is one, and of that there is nothing to be said. God works, the Godhead does no work: there is nothing for it to do, there is no activity in it…God and Godhead are distinguished by working and not working[4]…When I enter the ground, the bottom, the river and fount of the Godhead, none will ask me whence I came or where I have been. No one missed me, for there God *unbecomes*.[5]

This passage could have flowed directly from the source of the Vedas or Krishna's discourse in the *Gita*. While (as part of the trinity that is Ishwara) Brahma is the creator God who acts in the phenomenal world, *Brahman* is the "God beyond" whom we may never know by sense or reason. And yet it is this

---

3. Blakney, 134, which *should* also be Sermon 36, Walshe; however, I cannot find a comparable passage in either Sermon 36 or 37 (the sermons on "Adolescens, tibi dico: surge") in Walshe, which leads me to infer that Blakney was using some of his putative literary license in paraphrasing the Meister (albeit, in the correct *spirit* of the Meister).
4. I rather prefer Blakney's elegant phrasing, "The difference between God and the Godhead is the difference between action and nonaction." (Blakney, 226)
5. Eckhart, Sermon 56, *Sermons*, 2:81-82. .

Brahman which is "that": the Atman, the very nature of our souls, and, in fact, in all that exists.

"This entire universe is pervaded by me, in that eternal form of mine which is not manifest to the senses," Krishna states in Chapter IX. "Although I am not within any creature, all creatures exist within me. I do not mean that they exist in me personally. That is my divine mystery."[6]

But the element of mystery, the unknowable nature of the Godhead, is no obstacle for the seeker committed to the path of mysticism. "Mystery is horrible to us," observes Underhill[7], and it is precisely the *mystic* as opposed to any other human type who has both the inclination and the desire to undertake and complete the training necessary to tackle mystery head on and get the knowing that can be obtained in no other way. This path is "easy," Krishna states, presaging the words of Christ: "My yoke is easy and my burden is light" (Matt. 11:30). Underhill adds that mysticism is a practical path for the active person and involves "a training of his latent faculties, a bracing and brightening of his languid consciousness, an emancipation from the fetters of appearance, a turning of his attention to new levels of the world."[8]

As revealed in the opening half of the *Gita*, Krishna offers a program and methodology for Arjuna and all those (active people or not) who would know their place in the universe and seek its deepest meaning. According to Sri Aurobindo (1872-1950, Indian scholar and Yoga master), in Chapter IX the Lord takes a "turn of the greatest importance"[9] by showing that the vision of God (to be revealed in all its glory in Chapter XI) can only be known by the seeker who follows the yoga of mysticism.

This mystical perspective is captured in one of Eckhart's most celebrated statements: "Wiltu den kernen haben, so muostu die schalen brechen," translated as, "If you would have the kernel, you must break the shell."[10] The "nutcracker," if you will, that Krishna recommends to the seeker who would break

6. *Gita*, 101.
7. Underhill, 4.
8. Underhill, 6.
9. Sri Aurobindo, opening notes to *Bhagavad Gita and its Message*, 142.
10. Eckhart, Sermon 11b, *Sermons*, 1:83.

through to the Ground is the path of renunciation, devotion, meditation, and total absorption in the divine.[11]

Krishna calls "fools" those who "pass blindly by the place of my dwelling here in the human form. And of my majesty, they know nothing at all, who am the Lord, their soul."[12] Those ignorant of their essential nature are in the grasp of what Underhill calls "the crowd-spirit,"[13] the garrulous, outward-looking human personality in love with appearances and afraid of the unknown desert that looms within. But in much of his later vernacular work, Eckhart does not distinguish between the person living in the world and the recluse depriving him or herself of immersions in the activities of everyday life. To him, mysticism is so central an experience and fact of life that it joyfully pervades the life of the seeker at all times and in all places, lifting him or her above the ordinary into an extraordinary encounter with the divine. The desert darkness he describes is not life-negating, but Life-affirming, a space infinitely more illuminating than light, described in negative terms only because it is beyond even our most glorious imaginings. The paradoxes for which the language of the Meister and so many other mystics are famous abound in his attempts to depict the profound insights to which anyone may be privy. Whether monk or what the Hindu would call *householder*, the seeker who follows the mystic's path opens him or herself up to being taken over and operated by the Absolute. Eckhart preaches:

Let go of yourself and let God act with you and in you as He will. This work is His, this Word is His, this birth is His, in fact every single thing that you are. For you have abandoned self and have gone out of your (soul's) powers and their activities, and your personal nature. Therefore God must enter into your being and powers, because you have bereft yourself of (attachment to) all possessions, and become as a desert, as it is written: "The voice of one crying in

---

11. And, as Krishna declares, it can indeed be easy...for the person who knows how to use it! A skilled cracker of nuts can split the shell in a single crunch. A less experienced person, without the "feel" for nut and instrument, is likely to wind up with a pile of shards in his or her hands, and possibly some nicked fingers.
12. *Gita*, 103.
13. Underhill 77.

the wilderness" (Matt. 3:3). Let this eternal voice cry out in you as it listeth, and be as a desert in respect of yourself and all things.[14]

By consecrating all things to God, we make them holy, states Krishna, who, in a bold display of ecumenism, declares that sacrifices made to any deities will go to those deities, and those who believe fully in, say, ancestor worship or elemental spirits will in fact go to their ancestors or these spirits when they die.[15] And while devotion and love are keys to unlocking the divine mystery within, yet the non-dual, eternal Brahman is beyond love and hate, embracing all within his formless Being. In a statement that resonates with the teachings of Christianity, he declares, "Though a man be soiled with the sins of a lifetime, let him but love me, rightly resolved, in utter devotion: I see no sinner, that man is holy."[16]

The yoga of mysticism leads the seeker to the realization that "the countless gods are only my million faces,"[17] and sets the stage for the revelations of divine glory and the vision of God in His universal form which comprise the most awe-inspiring poetry of the *Gita* and offer the seeker some small suggestion of the explosive Power that Eckhart states is given birth eternally in the soul of each individual woman and man.

---

14. Eckhart, Sermon 3, *Sermons,* 1:33.
15. *Gita,* 107.
16. Ibid.
17. Ibid., 104

10

Divine Glory

Reading the tenth chapter of the *Gita*, and the chapter called "The Vision of God" which follows it, one encounters a world which would be familiar to many European medieval mystics and artists: a world where the imagination is untrammeled in its expression of the glory of God. This is a world where words can at least attempt to convey the wonder of the Absolute in concrete terms intelligible to seekers such as Arjuna, a universe filled with dazzling images reminiscent of the depictions of the heavenly realms by anonymous medieval Western artists, the icon painters of Russia and Greece, and those of the pre-or early Renaissance (Giotto and his followers).

After the austerity and intellectual banter of the first half of the *Gita*, Chapter X bursts forth with radiant sensuosity. "I am where all things began," intones Krishna (sounding more and more like Ishwara or Yahweh). I am "the issuing-forth of the creatures, known to the wise in their love when they worship with hearts overflowing...[I am] that brilliant lamp, dispelling its darkness."

After accepting some worshipful words from Arjuna (and a little encouragement), the Lord goes on to reveal Himself as:

• The radiant sun,

• The wind-god,

• "...among the stars of night, I am the moon..."

• consciousness of the living,

• the spirit of fire,

• the ocean,

• the godly sage and the celestial musician,

• God's thunderbolt, the heavenly cow, the love-god, the god of snakes,

• Lion, shark, the River Ganges,

"I am Time without end: I am the Sustainer: my face is everywhere,"[1] he declares. "I am the divine seed of all lives."[2]

This vivid, awe-inspiring portrait, familiar to the Western medieval mind, is not found explicitly in the preaching of Meister Eckhart. The medieval men and women to whom Eckhart addressed his sermons and instructions already were immersed in an image-rich environment where God was depicted not only in the form of his Son, but also as the Father and sometimes as the Holy Ghost (a dove). Churches were crammed with artifacts designed to lift the consciousness of the faithful to visions of heaven which were as concrete and emotionally charged as the objects of their day-to-day existence. Churches as well as cathedrals were decorated with depictions of holy scenes, often the only way to convey Biblical teachings to a largely illiterate public. Scenes in which divine nature (either expressed through saints or in God Himself) was variously depicted as the ocean, heavens, and members of the animal kingdom, would have been commonplace in the medieval world. But they were not common in the teachings of Meister Eckhart, though they may have been implicit in his mystical understanding of the cosmos.

The proliferation of sensuous images to suggest deity speaks to a deep human need to understand the abstract first in terms of the concrete. Huston Smith quotes a telling anecdote about C.S. Lewis to this effect:

> Most people, however, cannot be gripped by such high-order abstractions. That C.S. Lewis is among their number is proof that their minds are not inferior, only different. Professor Lewis tells us that while he was a child his parents kept admonishing him not to think of God in terms of any form, for these could only limit his

---

1.   *Gita*, 114-16.
2.   Ibid., 117.

infinity. He tried his best to heed their instructions, but the closest he could come to the idea of a formless God was an infinite sea of grey tapioca.[3]

Well, the formless God certainly was not grey tapioca to the great Dominican! So enraptured was Eckhart by the formless Presence, which there is no doubt he personally experienced as a living reality, that all phenomenal comparisons, metaphors, agents, and descriptors dropped like lifeless weights from his inventive mind and powerful vocabulary. While at times he uses similes or Bible stories to help his listeners understand or to drive home a point, in general his prose is terse, intimate, and largely cheerful. He recognizes that finite human speech cannot be stretched to describe or convey the infinite glory of God. There are exceptions, of course, as when he attempts to describe heaven (also cited in Chapter VII of this book):

> All creatures God ever created or might yet create, if He wished, are little or nothing compared with God. Heaven is so vast and so wide that if I told you, you would not believe it. If you were to take a needle and prick the heavens with it, then that part of heaven that the needle-point pricked would be greater in comparison to heaven and the whole world, than heaven and the world are compared with God.[4]

This is an apt comparison, but it doesn't rate as one of the Meister's more memorable declarations. In fact, compared with the poetic diction of the *Gita*, where Krishna starts at the level of a hum and swells to the kind of roar that makes your hair stand on end, it's frankly boring. But this is because to Eckhart, trying to describe the Absolute in material terms was an exercise, not only in futility, but in impossibility as well. God (and certainly the Godhead) has no properties. If He is, like Krishna, to be likened to the sun, it must be implied, not stated directly by this master of apophatic mysticism. An example of this obliqueness can be found in Sermon 67: "But the man who would come to that of which I have been speaking (mystical union)...should be like the

---

3.   Huston Smith, *The World's Religions*, (New York and San Francisco: HarperSanFrancisco, 1991), 61.
4.   Eckhart, Sermon 42, *Sermons*, 1:293-4.

morning star: for ever present to God and by Him, at an equal distance, and raised above all earthly things, a 'by-word' beside the Word." Humanity's morning star follows God's sun. But God is not openly referred to as the sun; in fact, the word "sun" is never used.

Eckhart preached and wrote in an era notable for the vivid spiritual imagery of its Churches, mystics, writers, and artists, who reveled in gruesome depictions of Christ's agony and victory, ghastly images of hell's horrors, and opulent portrayals of paradise's gold-leaf glory. Despite Eckhart's incomparable command of language, a clever mind, and both an understanding and love of people of every ilk, there is none of this magic in the wonderful web he spins. His web looks more to us like the gossamer of space, all etched in black and white, where sheer, twisted galaxies a billion stars strong stretch their kinetic lace over infinite black eternity. It *looks* impersonal, if we try to objectify it thus. And yet it penetrates deep into the Ground of the Soul where only the most single-minded *love* can lead. And so Eckhart, beloved of those who eschew emotionalism and passion in religion, turns the tables in his typically paradoxical style, for it is love alone, the most unstable and highly charged of all spiritual operatives, that lifts the seeker into an indescribable realm of bliss beyond anything our feeble human emotions can ever feel or know. "Abandon yourself to God in utter faith and perfect love, then *whatever* is born in you or touches you, within or without, joyful or sorrowful, sour or sweet, that is no longer yours, it is altogether your God's to whom you have abandoned yourself."[5] Despite the dearth of sensuous imagery in the Meister, McGinn states that Eckhart does *not* want his listeners to understand God in an abstract sense, but rather experience "the reality of what it means to live in this awareness,"[6] the awareness of nothingness and self-abandonment.

Even in the middle period of life, the Meister admonishes monks to give up "*internal* imagery, whether it be in the form of pictures or lofty thoughts, or outward impressions or whatever is present to his mind, nor be distracted nor dissipate himself in their multiplicity. A man should train and bend all his powers to this and keep his inner self present to him."[7] The spiritual seeker must be liberated of all images. "And therefore there must be a silence and a stillness, and the Father must speak in that, and give birth to His son, and per-

---

5. Ibid., Sermon 3, 1:32.
6. McGinn, 232.
7. Eckhart, *The Talks of Instruction, Sermons,* 3:45.

form His works free from all images."[8] And again, "...forget all those things and their images which you have absorbed...the further you can get from creatures and their images, the nearer you are to this and the readier to receive it."[9] Clearly, this is not because Eckhart is a killjoy and spoilsport who delights in robbing simple minds of their images, but rather because, as the coach for a number of spiritual teams, it is his responsibility to lead them to the bliss of victory over ignorance and delusion and the unparalleled experience of plunging into their own true Nature.

But even Eckhart, dealing as he is with mortals who may not venture far without some phenomenological reassurances, occasionally dips into the language of the flowering, flowing world to entice his listeners into deeper practice. "...there is a power in the soul which touches neither time nor flesh, flowing from the spirit, altogether spiritual," he declares in Sermon 8. "In this power, God is ever verdant and flowering in all the joy and all the glory that He is in Himself. *There* is such heartfelt delight, such inconceivably deep joy as none can fully tell of..."[10]

And even the Lord Krishna, with his plethora of vivid imagery, calling Himself the beginning, middle, and end of creation; the source of all that is born; the very jaws of death...even this Lord concludes his discourse with a statement of Eckhartian starkness and simplicity:

> But what use have you, Arjuna, to know this huge variety? Know only that I exist, and that one atom of myself sustains the universe.[11]

---

8. Ibid., Sermon 1, 1:6.
9. Ibid, 1:7.
10. Ibid., Sermon 8, 1:74.
11. *Gita*, 117.

11

The Vision of God in His Universal Form

Creator, Preserver, Destroyer—these are the three faces of Ishwara in the Hindu Trinity, the form that Arjuna now asks to see. How different from the Trinity that Meister Eckhart so often references in his sermons and treatises, the paradigm of the Father Creator, the Son who is God incarnate, and the Holy Spirit, the living but invisible Presence that dwells in human hearts. The Indian spiritual tradition, extending back in time perhaps 10,000 years, exemplifies a holistic view of the universe in which all aspects of being, negative as well as positive, are included, accepted, supported, and accounted for. The Christian view is not less complete, but in general presents a dualist perspective. Here is the Good: God, expressed in His Trinity. There is evil, an aberration, deprivation of the good, Lucifer's dark and dangerous lark, not comparable to the supreme Lord and His operations. Shiva, Ishwara as destroyer, is viewed as powerful force, the archetype of the wild man, but being fully divine is not the Indian equivalent of Satan. The same God who creates and preserves all existence is responsible for its destruction and resurrection over and over again, offering a cyclical vision of time in counterpoint to Christianity's chronological, progressive perspective.

The concept of Trinity in both Eastern and Western traditions provides an interesting hook for a discussion of God's universal Form. Both the Hindu tradition and Eckhart go one step further, however, into the realm of Brahman or the distinctly Eckhartian interpretation of *gotheit* (Eckhart, in this case, venturing boldly where few Catholics had gone before). And there is

another element that they have in common, though they use it very differently. This is the use of visceral shock to startle the sluggish, *tamasic* seeker
into a hair-raising experience of that which words alone could never convey. It
is worth looking at each of these dissimilar similarities more closely.

When Krishna responds "just this one time" to Arjuna's plea to see the
divine glory, he does not plunge directly into a revelation of *savikalpaka samadhi* (total absorption in Brahman with consciousness of one's own being) and
nirvikalpaka samadhi (total absorption without distinctions).[1] Arjuna, *rajasic*
action-oriented individual that he is, is not yet ready for this sublime immersion. Instead, Krishna continues to interact with Arjuna on the phenomenal
level, revealing the creative power, majesty, and decimating horror of the Tri-
une God in a series of psycho-sensual exhibitions that take human consciousness to the last frontier of possibility.

Krishna imbues Arjuna with divine sight to see all the gods within His
body, utterly without limit, "infinite of arms, eyes, mouths and bellies...mil-
lion-armed, the sun and moon your eyeballs, firey-faced, you blast the world
to ashes."[2] At the same time, the dark side of God appears, "terrible with
fangs...mouths agape and flame-eyes staring...with frightful tusks your
mouths are gnashing, flaring like the fires of Doomsday morning..."[3] Heroes
tumble into His hideous jaws "where mangled heads lie crushed between
them!"[4]

To Arjuna's trembling "Who are You?", Krishna intones the celebrated
lines,

I am come as Time, the waster of the peoples,
Ready for that hour that ripens to their ruin.[5]

Do not worry about slaying those who will come to me thus in the end, the
Lord says. As you can see, they are already as dead men. Therefore, bravely
perform your duty.

---

1. These definitions are taken from Swami Harshananda, *A Dictionary of
    Advaita Vedanta* (Bangalore, India, 1990).
2. *Gita*, 120-21.
3. Ibid, 121-2.
4. Ibid.
5. Ibid., 123.

Arjuna lies prostrate, a quaking shadow of his former magnificent self. Krishna withdraws the vision of his fearsome majesty and reassures the youth that He has shown him this visage out of love and tenderness. One may see the divine Shape "not by study of the Vedas, nor by austerities, nor by alms-giving, nor by rituals," he declares (words to be echoed in Eckhart in another place and another time[6]).

As discussed in Chapter X, one will find *vivid images* of heaven and hell throughout the medieval world, but will look in vein for similar images in Eckhart. In his work, the chaotic world with its multiplicity of forms yields to a simple presence, haunting in its familiarity. Eckhart knows that humans are weak, and surely would have considered himself as fallible as any (his *Defense*, although provided under coercive circumstances, attests to the Meister's humility, in this writer's opinion). But even so, *why take an intermediate step*, as other mystics allow? For Eckhart, there is no reincarnation to "work things out." He enjoins his listeners to take the plunge now right into the heart of God, beyond phenomenal images and media, and seek the birth already taking place there, unbeknownst to them. And while Eckhart may be averse to the use of vivid pictorial images, he speaks frequently of a single divine image impressed upon the soul, an image that be intuited rather than seen.

According to Eckhart, there is an irresistible reciprocity between God and the soul. It is God's nature to empty into a virtuous soul, and conversely, it is the soul's nature to receive God. "…the soul bears God's image and is like God," states Eckhart,[7] but the soul is not a likeness of God. It is, so to speak, "the real thing," not a copy or reflection. By way of analogy, Eckhart states that two eggs are alike in that they are similarly white. But you couldn't say that one egg is the image of the other. In order to become the image of some-thing, an object must have "come from its nature and be born of it and be like it."[8] But Eckhart declares unequivocally that the soul is *not* God Himself. If that were the case, "God would not be God," he continues.[9] And yet there is a

---

6. "If someone knows himself to be well trained in true inwardness, then let him drop all outward disciplines, even those he is bound to," writes Eckhart. This sentence is quoted in Chapter III of this study, from McGinn, 69, quoting from his translation of Sermon 104 (Walshe's Sermon 4).
7. Eckhart, Sermon 14b, *Sermons*, 1:123-4..
8. Ibid., 124.
9. Ibid., 125.

relationship between God and the soul which is unfathomably intimate. Something which is the image of another takes its being from that other; in fact, it is the same *being*. So the soul may not be God Himself, but it shares in His being, a conclusion that would not surprise Arjuna, but certainly set a certain coterie of the ecclesiastical hierarchy of 14th century Europe on its collective ear.

Eckhart goes on to draw several conclusions about the image of God impressed on the soul:

* An image is not of itself or for itself;

* It belongs solely to God, That whose image it is;

* The soul does not belong to anything that is *alien* to God (in the Christian tradition, this would be evil or the forces of darkness);

* There is no "means" or operation whereby the soul derives its image from God;

* The soul shares an essence with God: it is the *same* essence.[10]

Although Eckhart takes a different approach than the *Gita* to the use of imagery in conveying the majesty of the divine, he and Krishna share a similar didactic message. After revealing the divine form, Krishna tells Arjuna (and all humanity) to work for God alone, make Him your only goal, and be devoted to God with detachment and without hate for any creature. Likewise, Eckhart tells his listeners,

> You often ask how you ought to live. Now pay close attention. Just as I have told you about the image—that is the way you should live! You should be His and for Him, you should not be your own or for yourself, or belong to anyone…the good man…draws from the same source as the Son, and is himself the Son…if you would know God, you must not merely be *like* the Son, you must *be* the Son."[11]

10. Ibid., 126.
11. Ibid., 127.

This last statement shocks and astonishes us even today. It is as sharp as a blow from the master's stick in a Rinzai zendo. As Arjuna trembles, his hair standing on end, at the fierce revelation Krishna bestows, so Eckhart's listeners would have reeled to hear the Meister drop into their consciousness words that seemed to shatter every conventional thought they'd ever had about their relationship to the sublime. There is no room here for imitation: you must *be* (not even *become*!) the very Son of God, the image born of the Father (not a reflection or likeness). You must acknowledge God's emptying out into you and recognize who you are, or why bother to pretend that you care about your kinship to the divine at all?

Time and again, Eckhart resorts to these shock techniques to jolt our consciousness and force us to confront the raw facts of God's being in us. Amazing lines leap from his sermons, telling monks to toss out their vows, informing laypeople that they are one with God, advising seekers to forget about God and find the Source that hides behind the linguistic construct. We are left dizzy, confused, separated from the safety net of conventional religious teaching, which is more concerned with keeping us safe than making us free. These are the birth pains of liberation, and both Krishna and Eckhart are the midwives coaching us through our own new birth.

12

The Yoga of Devotion

Asked by Arjuna which is the better route to God, disinterested worship or love, Krishna gives a surprising answer:

> Those whose minds are fixed on me in steadfast love, worshipping me with absolute faith, I consider them to have the greater understanding of yoga.

This is surprising considering the emphasis Krishna has placed on detachment and renunciation of sensuous distractions. But it not the emotional love of *eros*, or the intellectual love of *agape* which Krishna means. The Sanskrit term, *bhakti*, has a unique connotation, suggesting the giving up of self in pure devotion to and absorption in the higher power. According to Swami Gnaneswarananda, a follower of Swami Vivekananda of the Ramakrishna Order, all emotion may be resolved into this kind of love. And, in fact, the love itself *is* God.

> The highest goal in bhakti yoga is infinite love, or God. Bhakti yoga regards man's natural power of love as a manifestation of the divine within and teaches him to purify that love until it becomes omnipotent. By perfecting, magnifying, and extending the spark of love we have within us, we are enabled to realize God, who is infinite love. God is love; love is God.[1]

---

1.   Swami Gnaneswarananda, *Yoga for Beginners* (Chicago: Vivekananda Vedanta Society, 1975), 118.

Citing Chapter XII if the *Gita*, Gnaneswarananda lists the main characteristics of the *bhakta* as purity, loyalty, trust, and spontaneous devotion. The *bhakta* progresses through various stages until there is an absolute negation of self, "and love alone exists," in what is known as *prema yoga*. "*Prema* leads to the consummation of *bhakti*, or *bhava samadhi*, the goal of *bhakti* yoga."[2]

As quoted in Chapter III of this study, Eckhart, too, embraces this definition of love as complete surrender to God when he enjoins seekers to "...put on the bridle of love!...God lies in wait for us with nothing so much as with love...the more you are caught, the more you are free."[3] When one considers the word, "love," as a synonym for God, it is not so difficult to understand how absolute negation of self could create space for love to enter in and empty itself in the soul. One is reminded of George Herbert's poem, *Love*, so beloved of the 20th century mystic Simone Weil,

LOVE bade me welcome: yet my soul drew back,

Guiltie of dust and sinne.

But quick-ey'd Love, observing me grow slack

From my first entrance in,

Drew nearer to me, sweetly questioning,   5

If I lack'd any thing.

A guest, I answer'd, worthy to be here:

Love said, you shall be he.

I the unkinde, ungratefull? Ah my deare,

I cannot look on thee.   10

Love took my hand, and smiling did reply,

Who made the eyes but I?

---

2.   Ibid., 123.
3.   Eckhart, Sermon 4, *Sermons*, 1:46.

Truth Lord, but I have marr'd them: let my shame

Go where it doth deserve.

And know you not, sayes Love, who bore the blame?   *15*

My deare, then I will serve.

You must sit down, sayes Love, and taste my meat:

So I did sit and eat.*

* Public domain, see http://www.bartleby.com/105/

The *bhakti*, emptied of all nourishment and hungry for the divine presence, is "served," as in Herbert's poem, by the Being who is Love Himself. In an offering which helps us make sense of the Christian mystery of Holy Communion, God serves up Himself to us if we are empty of ourselves and surrender to his Presence.

For Eckhart, Christ's message, which can be summarized as, "Love is all you need,"[4] is a familiar staple of his spiritual diet as a Christian monk. Likening divine love to fire, Eckhart suggests that the Holy Spirit acts as the wind fanning its flame. "The greater the love that is in the soul, and the more the Holy Ghost breathes on it, the more perfect the flame: but this does not happen all at once, but gradually with the growth of the soul. For if a man were to catch fire too suddenly, that would not be a good thing. Therefore the Holy Ghost breathes gradually on the flame, so that a man, even if he were to live for a thousand years, would still increase in love."[5] It is interesting that the same symbol—fire—is used for both consumption by Divine Bliss and damnation by eternal hellfire. But for Eckhart, as we have seen earlier, the horrors of hell are no incentive to seek the Absolute, whose own mercy, compassion, and consuming love are reason enough to let go of sense attachments and open up to possession by the Holy.

Eckhart seems to find no disconnect between loving and detachment. However, speaking to Arjuna, Krishna suggests that these are two distinct paths, and that his recommendation of *bhakti yoga* is based on the difficulty

---

4. A tip of the hat to the Beatles is in order.
5. Eckhart, Sermon 62, *Sermons*, 2:113.

most people have (especially active types like Arjuna) following disciplines such as objectless awareness and staying on track for the long haul. Krishna knows the fallible, weak nature of mortals, and offers a series of options. If you fail to become absorbed in Him, try concentration. If that fails, devote yourself to good works to please Him. If you can't do even this, just let go and surrender yourself to God.[6]

Krishna then recounts the qualities of those who aspire to this loving practice (as well as the effects that this practice will have on them). The follower of *bhakti yoga* must "hate no living creature," is compassionate, and friendly, free of delusion. United with God, he or she is detached, dispassionate, and self-controlled. "His home is everywhere and nowhere," he says,[7] reminiscent of Jesus's comment that the Son of Man has nowhere to lay his head. The key, he repeats, is renunciation followed by complete surrender.

Some have taken Krishna's words to imply that devotion is a second-rate path to realization, since those with a higher level of attainment would have the self-discipline to concentrate on the Unmanifest. Yet neither the *Gita*'s narrative nor Eckhart's instructions requires this explanation. Rather they challenge our understanding of "love," giving us a reading of "devotion" which is richer and deeper than the popular meaning of this multi-faceted concept. Love is, in fact, not only the nature of God, but it is also the means with which He takes us as His own. Eckhart uses the metaphor of a fish catcher's hook to explain this:

> The fisherman cannot get the fish until it is caught on the hook. Once it takes the hook, he is sure of the fish: twist and turn as it may, this way or that, he is assured of his catch. And so I say of love: he who is caught by it has the strongest of bonds and yet a pleasant burden. He who has taken up this sweet burden fares further and makes more progress than by all the harsh practices any (people) use…Nothing brings you closer to God or makes God so much your own as the sweet bond of love. A man who has found this way need seek no other. He who hangs on this hook is caught so fast that foot and hand, mouth, eyes and heart, and all that is man's, belongs only to God.[8]

---

6.   *Gita*, 129.
7.   Ibid., 130-31.
8.   Eckhart, Sermon 4, *Sermons*, 1:46-47.

Nothing is more useful than love to the seeker who would advance beyond the limits of the senses, the Meister says. With its focus on the Field (the phenomenal world) and its Knower, Chapter XIII of the *Gita* juxtaposes the power of devotion against the distractions of *Prakriti*, two concepts not unfamiliar to Eckhart. Here, the *Gita* provides some practical advice that throws light on some of Eckhart's own instructions.

13

The Field and Its Knower

In response to Arjuna's question, Krishna states that the Field is the world of sense objects, and God is the Knower. But it is not as simple as that, for men and women are neither wholly one nor the other, at least in Arjuna's own limited perception. Krishna says that he is the Knower in every body, but each person also, at a certain level, stands apart from the Field and has the power to think about it as though it were a separate entity. A person on a diet, for example, experiences hunger and desire in the Field, but also may hear a higher voice admonishing him not to eat cake for the term of the regime. Is this the voice of God, a subtle form of our own material self-interest, or simply conscience? And what of the person following a virtuous life who experiences an overwhelming impulse to do something inappropriate, such as steal a car? Is this an intervention from an unconventional divinity, a temptation from a devil or *mala*, or merely one of those troublesome *vritti* that Patanjali rails against as obstacles to mental calm?

But subtlety is wasted on our warrior hero, Krishna seems to reflect, and so the Lord of the Universe launches into a no-frills discourse on the difference between the earthly and the divine. His conclusion, that Brahman is the power of seeing in the eyes, hearing in the ears, and feeling in the skin, sets a context for Eckhart's powerful thesis that all that God is, is being, and, of His knowing, that all that He knows is being.

"God knows nothing but being, He is conscious of nothing but His being: being is His circumference."[1] And here he parts company with the Hindu

---

1.   Eckhart, Sermon 82, *Sermons*, 2:244.

Lord, at least at this stage of explication, flying off in typically Eckhartian manner to a speciously outrageous declaration: "I say all creatures are one being." Few statements in Eckhart sound so boldly Vedantic, so unequivocal in their absolute conviction of unity and nondualism. Eckhart goes even further, disagreeing with an unnamed master who claimed that some creatures were so close to God that they carried off some of His light and could pass it on to others. "That is not true," he states earnestly, and one can imagine him squinting his blue eyes and leaning over the lectern to catch the gaze of his enrapt audience, "for being is so high, so pure and so akin to God that no one can give being save God alone in Himself."[2] And then, "So far as our life is one being, so far it is in God." To know the meanest thing in God as it is one being is better than to know an angel, he whispers. Being is the highest good, and the highest state of being—in God—must be the goal of every living soul. As we are part of God, God's knowing is our knowing, and God's being is our own.

Krishna states that it is the Knower who illumines the Field:

> By the single sun
> This whole world is illumined:
> By its one Knower
> The Field is illumined.[3]

Eckhart would have no argument with this, but would startle us into the realization that the consciousness of the Knower is not any different from the consciousness of those "toiling" in the Field. Knowledge, not will (as the Franciscans argued) leads us to an understanding of the cause of being, and shows us that being is undivided. "...life can never be perfected till it returns to its productive source where life is (the) one being that the soul receives when she dies right down the 'ground,' that we may live in that life wherein life is one being."[4] This is an awesome statement, and not easy to grasp at first reading. It is easy to understand how some listeners, hearing this for the first time, or reading it in a transcript, might think that Eckhart was suggesting that there was no difference between a person and God.[5] Rather, Eckhart suggests that

---

2. Ibid.
3. *Gita*, 139.
4. Eckhart, Sermon 82, *Sermons*, 2:246.
5. Certainly, there is evidence that it was such misreadings that intrigued Nietzsche and later some of the Nazi apologists.

at the deepest level, the nature of the soul's being and God's being is one; but that God has the "upper hand," as it were, in that He is the source of being. One is reminded of Brahma the Creator continuously closing and opening an eye and creating yet another world in an endless and effortless concatenation of generative acts. Of course, for Hinduism, as for Eckhart, as we have seen earlier, there is another, unseen part of the story, one often called "negative," but only in the sense that it cannot be objectified. And that is the impersonal Brahman or *gotheit (Gottheit, Godhead)* which is the context in which this little drama unfolds.

The realm of the Field and its Knower extends not only over being, but also over time. In an earlier chapter, Krishna called time "the waster of the peoples...all these hosts must die."[6] Eckhart states that what holds us back from a full awareness of the infinite being we share with God is time, or rather our preoccupation and obsession with time. "Whatever touches time is mortal," he declares. "...the soul should be established in true being..."[7], not in time.

The other opponent men and women face in their search for union is the pairs of opposites. Eckhart lists them as a Taoist might: joy and sorrow, white and black, and their ilk act as a force field keeping us from the essential no-Thing. It makes one think of black and white magnets, in the shape of Scottie dogs, never being able to touch nose to nose because of the antagonism of conflicting electrical charges.

But reason and will, powers associated with the mind when ensconced in matter, fall away from the soul when she is liberated from the body. Is that liberation affected only by death? Some, whose hearts are purified, Krishna observes, realize the Atman within themselves in this very life through contemplation.[8] Eckhart says that this purification occurs when the soul is purified of a life *that is divided* and she enters into a life (not a death) of unity.[9] It is a life lived *beyond* time, an eternity in which death is as meaningless as the sloughed off skin of a snake. What is renounced in Eckhart's renunciation is addiction to opposites.

All that is scattered among lower things is united when the soul climbs up into a life where there are no opposites. When the soul enters the life of the

---

6. *Gita*, 123.
7. Eckhart, 2:246.
8. *Gita*, 137.
9. Eckhart, 2:247.

intellect, she knows no opposites. Whatever falls away from this light, falls into mortality and dies.[10]

Time, opposites...but there is a third obstacle men and women must overcome in order to meet and accept their divine destiny. This obstacle is objects, or, as the *Gita* would put it, the Field. Do not turn to any object, counsels the Meister. "Whatever is directed toward anything else must die and cannot subsist."[11]

With these words, Lord Krishna concludes his discourse on the Field and its Knower:

> Who thus perceives
> With the eye of wisdom
> In what manner the Field
> Is distinct from its Knower,
> How men are made free
> From the toils of Prakriti:
> His aim is accomplished,
> He enters the Highest.[12]

As though in a responsive reading, the Meister concludes his sermon in a complementary tone. "We pray to our dear Lord," he says, "to help us from a life that is divided into a life that is united. May God help us to do this. Amen."[13]

---

10. Ibid.
11. Ibid.
12. *Gita*, 139.
13. Eckhart, 2:247.

14

The Three Gunas

Three tendencies characterize the phenomenal world, variously referred to as *prakriti* (the world of the senses) or *maya* (illusion) in the *Gita*.[1] Usually described as traits or human types, the *gunas* actually are states inherent throughout the material plain. In Chapter XIV, Lord Krishna gives Arjuna a technical lesson in Hinduism basics, defining the three tendencies which make the world, and everything in it, go 'round.

The 20th century Vedantic sage, Swami Gnaneswarananda, describes the three *gunas* as follows:

- *Tamas*, characterized by dullness of mind, inertia, inadvertence, ignorance, and laziness;

- *Rajas*, which, despite its royal name, is associated with ego-central qualities such as lust, anger, arrogance, envy, and jealousy;

- *Sattwa*, expressed by absence of pride, faith, devotion to the search for truth, discrimination, and a strong yearning for liberation.[2]

---

1. *Prakriti* and *maya* are the same, according to Swami Gnaneswarananda, *Yoga for Beginners*, 21. The term *prakriti* is found more often in the Sankhya school of Hinduism, while the term *maya* appears in the School of Vedanta.
2. Gnaneswarananda, 31.

Even at their worst, the *gunas* seem to have merit in our lives. Without ignorance, how can we have enlightenment? Without lust, how would the human race continue? Without a strong yearning, why would we pursue a spiritual practice? To all appearances, the *gunas* seem to make it possible for people to live and better themselves. But despite some very positive-sounding qualities, especially in the tendency known as *sattwa*, the *gunas* are categorically dismissed by Krishna as obstacles. They are obstacles to truth, obstacles to awareness, obstacles to the realization of our true nature. "These are the bonds," he states, "that bind the undying dweller imprisoned in the body."[3]

In a sermon of disputed authenticity,[4] Meister Eckhart refers to a statement by Jesus in which the Lord says, "It is expedient for you that I go away, for if I go not away, you will not be able to receive the Holy Spirit" (John 16:7). Eckhart latches onto this image to talk about three types of people who are hindered in three different ways from realizing spiritual blessing. While these do not correspond exactly to the *gunas*, they show how hindrances to spiritual progress can surface in the most unexpected places. In fact, the more normal and routine they are, the more they keep us from unitive bliss.

The first category of people facing obstacles consists of sinful people who seek out pleasurable creature comforts rather than God. Heeding their animal instincts, they follow creatures and lose God in the bargain.

The first category is hardly surprising. But the second is as astonishing as hearing that the spiritual *sattwa* nature is an obstacle to enlightenment. The second hindrance, that keeps good people from true spirituality, is the Seven Sacraments! "The man who stops with the enjoyment of a symbol never comes to the inward truth, for all seven of these pieties refer to a single truth," Eckhart states. This statement is remarkable on several scores, but most notably in the treatment of the sacraments as symbols.[5] The Eucharist, for example, has never been regarded as a symbol by the Roman Catholic Church. To the Meister, however, anything that takes place in the world of material and sense

---

3. *Gita*, 141.
4. Blakney, *Meister Eckhart*, 197-202. This is not included in Quint nor in Walshe's translation based on Quint's transliteration of the *Deutsche Werke*.
5. Perhaps the strongest argument that this is *not* an Eckhart original lies in the fact that it is not included on this ground in Pope John XXII's Bull, "In agro dominico," the condemnation of articles in Eckhart's work issued after the Meister's death.

objects needs to be gotten past. He continues, "...to get no further than the symbol is to be kept from the one great truth." Communicants who are too zealous to receive the Lord's body in Communion "never receive it in reality. They expend too much diligence on superfluous things and are never joined to the truth—for truth is to be found within and not in visible phenomena."[6]

A third hindrance keeping good people back from perfection is becoming too dependent on images of Jesus Christ or laying too much stress of visions (not necessarily *visual* visions, but including mental images as well). In an age which valued visionary spirituality, Eckhart's comments about forsaking images (here and in other texts which are not disputed) strike a singular chord. It is especially noteworthy that many of the Meister's sermons were addressed to women nuns and *Beguines* who would have been most susceptible in the 13th and 14th centuries to visionary suggestion.[7]

Visions and inner voices often deceive us, Eckhart contends. This, he declares, is Christ's true meaning when he says he must go away. "By that he meant to speak...to all who want to be his disciples now and to follow him to higher perfection. His humanity is a hindrance to them in the pleasure with which they depend on him. If they are to follow God in all his ways, they must not follow the ways of any human being, for these will put them off the road to God,"[8] are the words of this attributed sermon. This last sentence is particularly problematic, possibly suggesting (at least in Blakney's translation) that Jesus is a human being, not God, although this, too, is not mentioned in the papal bull. Eckhart does not deny Christ's place in the Trinity, of course, and goes on in this sermon that Father and Son are "of one essence, God in person, Godhead in nature."[9]

---

6. Blakney, 198.
7. Not because they are women and therefore "more emotional," but rather because so many of the influential mystics of the medieval period, such as Hildegard of Bingen, Gertrud, the Mechtilds, Elizabeth of Schoenau, Julian of Norwich, Margery Kempe, et. al., were women and, for the most part, nuns or Beguines like themselves. Some of these women dictated or wrote of their experiences *after* Eckhart's life, but reflect attitudes already prevalent during his day. See Andrew Weeks, *German Mysticism from Hildegard of Bingen to Ludwig Wittgenstein*, (Albany: State University of New York Press, 1993), and Evelyn Underhill, *Mysticism*, (Guernsey, Channel Islands: The Guernsey Press Co., 1993).
8. Blakney, 200.
9. Ibid.

Eckhart's three hindrances are indeed quite different from the obstacles cited by Krishna, but their role is the same: preventing men and women from fulfilling their true nature as children of God. Krishna declares,

> A man is said to have transcended the *gunas* when he does not hate the light of sattwa, or the activity of rajas, or even the delusion of tamas, while these prevail; and yet does not long for them after they have ceased. He is like one who sits unconcerned, and is not disturbed..."[10]

Had he read these words, surely the Meister would have nodded his head in thoughtful agreement. "As long as a man has an object under consideration, he is not one with it," he says in this sermon. "Where there is nothing but One, nothing but One is to be seen."[11] Even good works, the Seven Sacraments, the image or vision of Jesus Christ, or other spiritual revelations will lead us astray if we do not press on and dive into "the barren Godhead, of which the Trinity is a revelation."[12] This brings to mind a sutra by the Hindu "father of Yoga," Patanjali, who wrote, "...paranormal perceptions are obstacles to attaining enlightenment if they distract and excite the mind." However, in the same sutra, Patanjali modifies this statement by adding, "Used properly, however, they help one overcome obstacles and lead to *samadhi*."[13] Eckhart would not agree with this modification, but the Hindu Lord seems to suggest as much when he recommends specific *tapas*, or austerity practices, to tame the senses and achieve a state of renunciation[14]. On the contrary, he enjoins seekers to "...cast out even the saints and angels and even our blessed Lady," continuing in a typically bold, sweeping statement, "because these are all

---

10. *Gita*, 145.
11. Blakney, 200.
12. Ibid.
13. Sutra III-38, *Threads of Yoga: The Yoga Sutras of Patanjali*. Like the *Gita*, the sutras are of generally unknown authorship, though attributed to the sage Patanjali. They were composed some time between the 4th century B.C.E. and the 4th century C.E., possibly the same time as the composition of the *Gita*.
14. As we saw in Chapter V, these practices include meditating on the third eye, engaging in breathing exercises, and holding the restless mind in check.

creatures!"[15] Few medieval mystics or even religious people of our own time would dare to make these declarations that the Meister makes time and again, always managing to catch us off guard and topple our assumptions. It is no wonder that scholars such as Shizuteru Ueda have pointed out many parallels between Eckhart's thought and method and that of Buddhism, especially in Rinzai Zen.[16]

Eckhart again uses the word "barren" to describe the Godhead, as he also uses words such as "desert" and "waste places" throughout his vernacular work. While these initially may conjure up negative images, they are in fact empty of imagery, like a dry fountain waiting to be filled with rainwater. Eckhart urges us to enter the unity of the Trinity, but to push ahead further "to the barren Godhead of which the Trinity is a revelation. In this barren Godhead, activity has ceased and therefore the soul will be most perfect when it is thrown into the desert of the Godhead, where both activity and forms are no more..."[17] Few concepts are less appealing to seekers, and it is a hard sell that Eckhart embarks upon. Even when spiritual practice is said to lead to extravagantly blissful states for the elect, most people would rather take the humdrum of everyday life than gamble it all on the unknown. But to state that what awaits us is not a heavenly city paved with gold but an empty wasteland "where activity and forms are no more" surely wins few new recruits to the path of renunciation.

But all is not what meets the eye on first viewing, and Eckhart's infinite perspective cannot be adequately communicated in our finite vocabulary. It is a desert where individual identity is destroyed and where an overwhelming sense of God's presence—absolutely beyond all description and characterization—inundates the soul in an experience of perfect unity. It is a wasteland where *delusion* (*maya*) of dualism is what shrivels up and blows away, and where divine realization floods the soul like living water. It is barrenness where our words utterly fail and we surrender as if deaf, blind, and unspeaking, to a power which lifts us up and takes us into Itself. "Then the soul neither works, nor knows, nor loves any more, but God through the soul works and knows and loves."[18]

15. Blakney, 200.
16. See Shizuteru Ueda, *Die Gottesgeburt in der Seele and der Durchbruch zur Gott: Die mystische Anthropologie Meister Eckharts und ihre Konfrontation mit der Mystik der Zen-Buddhismus*, (Gutersloh: Mohn, 1965).
17. Blakney, 200-201.
18. Blakney, 202.

Here, the person who has transcended the *gunas* "…rests in the inner calm of the Atman, regarding happiness and suffering as one. Gold, mud and stone are of equal value to him. The pleasant and the unpleasant are alike…He who worships me," Lord Krishna says, "with unfaltering love transcends these *gunas*. He becomes fit to reach union with Brahman,

> For I am Brahman
> Within this body,
> Life immortal
> That shall not perish:
> I am the Truth
> And the Joy for ever."[19]

---

19. *Gita*, 145.

15

Devotion to the Supreme Spirit

The image of the desert and wasteland, though prominent throughout Eckhart's work, is not entirely foreign to the *Gita*. The world as perceived by a spiritual seeker, Krishna continues in this chapter, can be likened to a fig tree. Rooted in heaven, its leaves are the songs of the Vedas, singing to all who will hear with empty hearts. Its earthward branches are fed by the *gunas*, its buds the things of the senses. "Roots it has also reaching downward into this world, the roots of man's action."[1]

Where we move from vegetative world into desert is the point where the seeker sharpens the axe of non-attachment and cuts through the firmly rooted tree. The tree must die to launch the seeker to a state of "no return to future births."[2]

Consider the following dialogue and venture to guess its context or source: "Oh, sir, must everything go then, and is there no turning back?"

---

1. This sentence, taken from the Prabhavananda-Isherwood translation, 147, becomes more comprehensible when read in the light of other translations: "...downward here into the world of men it plunges its roots of attachment and desire with their consequences of an endlessly developing action." (*Gita*, trans. Aurobindo, 15:2) And again, "...and its roots grow downwards, the bonds of action in the world of men." (*Gita*, trans. Besant, 15:2). The tree of phenomenal existence is described as being rooted in attachment and desire.
2. Ibid.

"No indeed, by rights there is no returning...if you give way to the impulse to turn back, you are bound to lapse into sin, and you may backslide so far as to fall eternally. Therefore there is no turning back, but only a pressing forward, so as to attain and achieve this possibility."

Except for the reference to "sin," this could be a continuation of Krishna's conversation with Arjuna. In fact, it is part of a discussion between Eckhart and a hypothetical brother on the subject of unknowing and embracing the darkness.[3] In response to his own question, "But what *is* this darkness? What do you call it? What is its name?", the Meister states that its only name is "potential receptivity," that is to say, the state of being which has the potential for allowing the soul to reach perfection. If the seeker turns back, it will be because of the magnetism of the senses, like the roots of Krishna's fig tree, draining soul-energy back into the heavy, imperfect earth. Pressing forward, however, "It (the intellect or soul) never rests until it is filled with all being."[4] At this point, in my reading of Eckhart's thought, darkness becomes a kind of radiant light; and since there is no duality in union, darkness and radiance are in fact one metaphor for the same unfolding.

Despite its harsh image of the felled tree, Krishna's discourse on devotion to the Supreme Spirit is luminous and filled with references to light.

> The light that lives in the sun,
> Lighting all the world,
> The light of the moon,
> The light that is in fire:
> Know that light to be mine.[5]

The Biblical texts Eckhart knew so well abound with references to light. From "Let there be light" in Genesis to "I am the Way, the Truth, the Light" in the Gospel of John, the Christian Bible likens the manifestation of divinity to the illumination of the eye which has been in darkness. It is not surprising, then, that a Dominican monk would transfer this use of imagery to his own preaching. Eckhart, however, is singularly imaginative and instructive in his use of light to explicate God's ineluctable pursuit and possession of the soul.

3.   Eckhart, Sermon 4, *Sermons*, 1:41.
4.   Ibid.
5.   *Gita*, 149.

For Eckhart, it is the intellect, not the will, which carries the seeker to his or her destiny with the divine. This intellect, though plunging ahead into what the English poet Henry Vaughan called "a dazzling darkness," can be likened to light finding a pathway to the glory of God. "The natural light of the intellect that God has poured into the soul is so splendid and so strong that all that God has created of bodily things seems mean and petty to it," Eckhart declares.[6] The Meister often refers to the light of the spirit or the point where God and the soul intersect as "a little spark" (vunklein).[7] Speaking metaphorically, God sends his angel to prepare and refine the soul that she (the soul) may receive this divine light. "God wraps and conceals Himself in the angelic light and is only waiting for a chance to creep out and give Himself to the soul," he states in a sermon sure to have appealed to the common people of his time.[8] "The angels that are so illumined (by flying into God's light) and so like God, draw God to them and suck Him in. I have said before, were I void and had this fiery inner love and likeness I should absorb God altogether," he adds in a breathtaking aside. "Light streams out and lights up what it falls on,"[9] he says, adding several sentences that tell us much about Eckhart's use of light imagery to convey God's permeating power:

> When we sometimes say a man is illumined, that means little. But when it bursts forth, that is far better: it breaks through into the soul and makes her like God and divine, as far as may be, and illumines her within. In this interior illumination she soars above herself in the divine light.[10]

But the light of the intellect, whether placed in the soul by God or through his angels, is not the only form of illumination that Eckhart addresses. A second form is the light of grace. "God's presence in the soul by grace brings in more light than any intellect can give: and all the light that intellect can give is but a drop in the ocean beside this light, indeed a thousandfold less," he states.[11] God continuously flows out into rational creatures with the light of

---

6. Eckhart, Sermon 73, 2:193.
7. Ibid., Sermon 8, 1:76.
8. Ibid., Sermon 48, 2:31
9. Ibid., 2:33.
10. Ibid., 2:34.
11. Ibid., Sermon 73, 2:194.

grace. "…we must approach this light of grace with our intellect to be drawn out of ourselves and ascend into that one light that is God Himself," he adds in another sermon.[12] Light, then, may be used to describe the intellect and grace, a power in the soul or indeed the very essence of God Himself. And yet, when all is said and done, the Godhead is beyond all imagery, beyond the images of darkness and light that flicker back and forth throughout Eckhart's writing and preaching, a kind of chiaroscuro of the spiritual realm, the ultimate and possibly the *only* state of being.

For all his emphasis on "no returning" in this chapter, Krishna has not been silent on the subject of light, using the metaphor to describe His own imperishability:

> This is my Infinite Being; shall the sun lend it
> Any light—or the moon, or fire? For it shines
> Self-luminous always: and he who attains me
> Will never be reborn.[13]

I am the "flame of life in all," the Lord persists, "I am in all hearts."[14] In a similar vein, Eckhart notes that "*Jesse* means a fire and a burning, and signifies the ground of divine love."[15] "The light that lives in the sun, lighting all the world, the light of the moon, the light that is in the fire: know that light to be mine," confides Krishna.[16]

Whether of intellect or grace, the mystery of light helps us to understand the God that cannot be known purely through reason and the senses. He is the God that can be approached only when these tools of the phenomenal world are put aside and we leap into His presence, as it were, at the speed of light. As light cannot be tasted or smelled or seen in and of itself, but makes all things visible and offers them up to our understanding, so God's uncontrollable love floods human lives when we turn our backs on insubstantial joys and focus our wholehearted attention on That which illumines all being.

---

12. Ibid., Sermon 88, 2:281.
13. *Gita*, 147.
14. Ibid., 149.
15. Eckhart, Sermon 61, *Sermons*, 2:109.
16. *Gita*, 149.

16

Divine and Demonic Tendencies

The light of the Spirit may be available to all, but men and women are unequally suited to recognize it, Krishna suggests in the sixteenth chapter of the *Gita*. There are, he states, two kinds of people: those born with divine tendencies, and those whose inclinations are decidedly "demonic."

Those with divine tendencies are "fearless and pure of heart," and display many wonderful qualities from an early age, such as charity, self-control, and faith.[1] Those with demonic tendencies can be identified by their conceit, anger, cruelty, and other unpleasant characteristics. Those with divine tendencies are bound for liberation. Those with demonic tendencies cruise in the general direction of further bondage. Writing this, the words of Psalm 1 come to mind. The delight of the godly person is "in the law of the Lord, and on this law he meditates day and night." The ungodly, in contrast, walks in the counsel of the wicked, stands in the way of sinners, and sits in the seat of mockers. The wicked are like chaff that the wind blow away, but the righteous receive the care and protection of God.

Though thoroughly versed in the Psalms, Eckhart takes a different approach to the presence of good and evil in humanity. Rather than divide them into teams, so to speak, he views the individual as a *person* divided, quite a modern point of view and in sync with modern psychology. "One should first know, and it is in fact obvious," he writes in *The Nobleman*, "that man has

---

1.   *Gita*, 151.

two kinds of nature: body and spirit." Quoting authorities from Origen to Isaac Israeli,[2] Eckhart suggests that there is an inner person and an outer person, a new person (spiritual and inward) and an old person (worldly and external). In one of Eckhart's creative interpretations of scripture, he equates the inner person with the aristocrat cited in the verse, "A nobleman went away to a distant country, and gained a kingdom for himself, and returned." (Luke 19:12). The new person has gained the kingdom of heaven through Christ. But in Eckhart's hand, this sentiment accrues a far from conventional Christian meaning.

As the person is divided, so are the spirits that attend upon each of us. A familiar image comes to mind of a person torn between the angel sitting on his or her right shoulder, and the devil on the left.[3] The evil spirit is in league with the outer person, while the angelic being supports inward strength. But despite the lure of the outward forces, there is a reason why we heed the voice of the nobleman calling us to virtuous choices. This is because God truly is within us. Not only is God within us in spirit, but His seed has been planted in us through the birth of the word in the soul. Using the metaphor of a wise gardener tending a fledgling plant, Eckhart suggests that a well tended "God seed" will grow into something much higher than human form. "The seed of a pear-tree grows into a pear-tree, that of a nut-tree into a nut-tree," he writes, "God's seed into God."

God's seed, in us, grows into God. What does this mean? Eckhart states many sensational things in his vernacular preaching, some of which may have been inspired outbursts that he would have had second thoughts about putting into print. But this treatise was written deliberately for publication. Eckhart has had time to think about the repercussions of recording his radical expression of spiritual truth as he experienced it. And yet he cannot hold back. The desire to communicate what he believes absolutely to be true and applicable for all people overshadows his own desire for safety and protection. Indeed, I feel that Eckhart believed so strongly in what he wrote that he *did* feel safe in expressing views that grated dangerously against more rigid interpretations of

2.   Israeli died in 933. Quint indicates that Israeli wrote a book titled, *Liber de Diffinitionibus*. It is worth noting that even while quoting widely accepted Western church fathers such as Augustine and Aquinas, Eckhart frequently quotes pagan, Jewish, and Islamic masters in his vernacular works.

3.   Left-handed readers may prefer to reverse the order.

church doctrine. He felt safe because he had lived the truth and could see nothing but good from its disclosure.

Eckhart goes on to expand even further on the idea that God's seed has been planted within us. The soul, like the scriptural nobleman, must go out from all forms and from himself if he really means to receive the Son. And here Eckhart adds a daring note, by adding, "...and *become* the Son in God's bosom and heart."[4] For in Eckhart, the Son of God is not a means to an end. "All that is 'means' is alien to God," he writes. "The divine nature is One, and each Person is also one and *is the same One that the (divine) nature is.*"[5] A person who would know God must become one with God. In fact, Eckhart suggests that union should come *before* finding the divine. "Be one, that you may find God!" he exhorts.[6] One wonders what an uneducated listener to this sermon would have thought of that admonition.

Returning to Krishna's discourse is to return to the sense that the Hindu Lord is, unlike Eckhart, aware of the limitations of his audience. Krishna addresses his teachings to an individual of simple motives, to one who does not have a background in theology or the fine points of spiritual practice. Krishna's doctrine unfolds in stages so Arjuna's mind can adjust to the enormity of his teaching. Eckhart's egalitarian spirit and impetuous nature operate against this approach. Whether speaking to fellow masters, to groups of professional religious, or to the lay public, Eckhart holds nothing back. "The man from whom God hid nothing," as he has been called, in turn would hide nothing from his listeners, whether or not they could understand. It is this spirit of openness and fairness that in part drew so many to Eckhart in his lifetime and, ironically, at the same time alarmed some church officials. In an age when heresy was punishable by death, how could they permit impassioned preaching that could inadvertently lead simple souls astray? It was not a question to concern the theocentric Meister until he stood before a tribunal in Avignon and recanted those articles that may have unintentionally harmed the people whose hearts he sought to touch and inspire.

---

4. Eckhart, "The Nobleman," in *Sermons*, 3:110.
5. Ibid. This idea is reinforced in the textbook of another religion whose originator was not familiar with either Eckhart or the *Gita*. In *Science and Health*, the 1910 edition, Chapter X, verses 27-29, Mary Baker Eddy states, "...there are not two bases of being, matter and mind, but one alone—Mind."
6. Ibid.

One of the ways in which Eckhart does stir the imagination of his listeners in *The Nobleman* is through his vivid descriptions of the divine. "…the first condition of felicity," he effuses, "is that the soul sees God *naked*." There is nothing standing between God and soul. Indeed, God has been stripped of his majesty and his mystery. He is all. There is nothing else. He is no-thing because he is every-thing that counts. As Eckhart states elsewhere, we must get beyond ideas about God, even ideas of his goodness and justice. "Therefore, strip God of all His clothing—seize Him naked in his robing-room where He is uncovered and bare in Himself. Then you will 'abide in Him.'"[7]

It is in knowing that we know God that we fulfill our kinship with Him. There is no blessedness for the inner person unless he or she is fully aware and cognizant of that knowing. Knowing is the supreme function of the intellect, and for Eckhart, the intellect is another word for soul, or essential being. Each person must look deeply within himself or herself and see, know, and experience one's connectedness. Quoting Ezekiel, Eckhart likens the noble person, the power within, to an eagle that soars, the highest and best, into the holy wilderness.[8]

At this stage, the demonic tendencies drop away like the illusion they have always been. "Let the scriptures be your guide," Krishna says kindly, "in deciding what you must do, and what you must abstain from." He who acts out of personal desire cannot reach the lofty goal. "First learn the path of action, as the scriptures teach it. Then act accordingly,"[9] he instructs, leading Arjuna to ask, at the onset of the next chapter, about the meaning of faith.

7. Eckhart, Sermon 63, *Sermons*, 2:118.
8. Eckhart, "The Nobleman," in *Sermons*, 3:114.
9. *Gita*, 154.

17

Three Kinds of Faith

Many thinkers have discussed the dichotomies inherent in faith and reason, few the links between faith and love. St. Paul is one of the few to address the relationship between these two virtues. "...if I have a faith that can move mountains, but have not love, I am nothing," he writes (I Cor. 13:2). But what is faith? Is it perhaps a component of love?

In reply to a question by Arjuna, Krishna suggests that there are three kinds of faith, associated with the three *gunas: sattwa, tamas*, and *rajas*. [1] As an individual's personality is constituted, so develops this style of faith. The godly *sattwa* worship the divine in its many guises, while the *tamas* worship the spirits of the dead and the *rajas* worship wealth and power. *Saddhus* who claim it is faith that drives them to punish and mutilate their bodies in fact are egoists and show-offs.[2] "In their foolishness, they weaken all their sense organs, and outrage me, the dweller within the body," he says.[3]

Motivated by their respective variety of faith, individuals pursue a path similarly colored by the *gunas*. Krishna describes the kinds of food are associated with the different *gunas* (fresh, juicy foods appeal to people of *sattwa* nature, for example). He goes on to comment on the activities associated with

---

1.   "Now listen!" advises Krishna at this point in the Prabhavananda-Isherwood translation of Chapter 17 of the *Gita*, using a rhetorical device that appears throughout Eckhart's sermons.
2.   Perhaps the attribution of this sentiment to Krishna reveals the influence of Buddhist moderation on Hinduism several centuries earlier.
3.   The *Gita*, 156.

the *gunas*, and even suggests that for people of *tamas*, their actions are so inert, hardly actions at all, that one could truthfully state that these are people of no faith whatsoever.

Meister Eckhart does not go into details about health and hygiene, food choices and personal preferences in worship. He is less concerned about our human foibles and tendencies and radiantly immersed in the Mind that is the source and true nature of all. Not surprisingly, rather than give us a personality-type-based discourse on faith, the Meister presents us with three definitions of love.

There are three kinds of love evidenced by Jesus, Eckhart tells his listeners, three types that we should strive to emulate.[4] Surprisingly, these are not the *agape, philos* and *storge* familiar to many Christians (or a fourth, *eros*, less esteemed by the conventional Church). Rather, the types of divine love Eckhart cites unfold in sequence and progression, and are characterized as natural, love by grace, and "God's love."

Natural love is God's irresistible love for beings. Through this love, He pours himself into all creatures with as much love as they can take, not favoring one creature over another. From this, Eckhart states, we learn to love all creatures equally. Even if we like some people more than others, we should at least have the same goodwill towards all.

The second form is love by grace. Here Eckhart uses one of his signature concepts, the idea of God flowing into the soul like a body of light. Through grace, God flows into the soul, and the soul itself receives this love. "…in the natural light man enjoys *himself*," states Eckhart, "but the light of grace, which is unspeakably more powerful, deprives man of self-enjoyment and draws him into itself."[5] Our natural, thinking intellect must be displaced by this loving light. When this occurs, we ascend above our everyday selves, and know and love God back as He is in Himself.

And the third kind of love is divine. Here the Meister returns to another of his signature concepts, the birth of the Son in the Ground of the Soul. He colorfully likens God to a woman in bed giving birth, but this birth is "(God's) understanding, eternally welling forth from (God's) paternal heart, in which lies all…joy."[6] Like the woman in childbirth, God loves nothing but His Son, "…for the Son is a light that has shone from all eternity in the Father's heart."

---

4.   Eckhart, Sermon 88, 2:279.

5.   Ibid., 2:281.

Linking together the three forms of love in one lyrical sweep, Eckhart uses the language of ascent to declare that we must climb (suggesting our own exertion) from the natural light (given to all creatures) into the light of grace (in which God pours Himself into us). Then, we must grow, not into a follower of the Son, but actually "into the light that is *the Son Himself.*"[7] Eckhart then involves the Trinity in his capstone statement on the perfection of these three loves.

> Thus we, by the love of the Holy Ghost, being unified into His Son, shall know the Father with the Son and love ourselves in Him and Him in ourselves with their mutual love.[8]

In continuing his discourse on the three kinds of faith, Krishna offers a practical path leading to the exalted experience of the divine. In this sermon, Eckhart, too, takes a practical bent. While Krishna suggests a *sattwic* path and recommends the use of mantras such as *Aum* and *Aum Tat Sat,*[9] Eckhart offers four progressive steps to those who would climb into the all encompassing light.

First, not unexpectedly, is detachment.

Second, is an active life whose ground is a soul filled with the Holy Spirit.

Third, is a life devoted to contemplation.[10]

Fourth, is an aspiring spirit, an eagerness to receive the blessing, even the transformation that God will work in each person who loves Him.

Without *faith*, states Krishna, all austerities, sacrifices, and rituals lose their meaning: they are unreal. Without *love*, Eckhart concludes, there is *no ladder to climb.* "For as long as a man is still on the ascent and receiving through the medium of creatures, he has not come to rest. But once he is climbing up into

---

6. Ibid., 282.
7. Ibid.
8. Ibid.
9. *Aum* is the sound most suggestive of blessedness and union. *Sat* means goodness or existence, while *Tat* means the Absolute.
10. Perhaps as a positive gesture toward the many women who responded to his words, Eckhart refers to the life of action as "the true life of Leah," and the life of contemplation as "the true life of Rachel." (Ibid., 282-283.) Eckhart used the story of Mary and Martha on many occasions to make similar points.

God, there in the Son he will receive with the Son the whole of what God has to give."[11]

The *Gita* seems to lead our hearts in a circle back to its initial premise just as Eckhart repeats the first step in an attempt to move toward a greater knowledge of the Holy. Detach. Be free of desire for lesser things. Or, to use the title of the *Gita*'s final chapter, embrace the Yoga of Renunciation.

---

11. Ibid., 283.

18

The Yoga of Renunciation (Again)

What is the difference between renunciation and nonattachment, Arjuna asks in this, the longest and last chapter of the *Gita*. The two principles, so identified by Prabhavananda-Isherwood, are translated differently in various editions. Sri Aurobindo has Arjuna ask what is the difference between the principle of Sannyasa and the principle of Tyaga. In a footnote, he interprets this as meaning the difference between outer and inner renunciation. Annie Besant calls the two elements "the essence of renunciation...and relinquishment."[1]

A seeker may renounce the world to all appearances, but be deeply attached to things, perhaps even holy things, in his or her inner life. A sage, on the other hand, may be surrounded by sensual delights and yet detached in the ground of his or her own being. Sannyasa is the "laying aside of desirable actions," but the preferred path is Tyaga, which lays aside the root of desire itself.[2]

Whether one thinks this distinction is significant or simply two ways of expressing the same thought, Arjuna's question can be likened to a cold stick of fine incense, inert and lifeless in and of itself. It is Krishna's multitextured response that sets the chapter on fire with fragrant meaning. Aurobindo's title, "The *Gunas*, Mind and Works," more accurately captures something of the

---

1.   *Gita*, 18th discourse, trans. Besant.
2.   *Gita*, trans. Aurobindo, 252.

scope of Krishna's culminating discourse. As seen in Chapter X of this study, Eckhart enjoins the professional religious to let go of all images and ideas that keep them from soaring heavenward. Krishna leads us along a path of thought often consonant with the teachings of the 14th century Dominican.

The distinction between two types of renunciation is not unlike Eckhart's concept of the detachment that we enforce with exertion (*Abgescheidenheit*) and the renunciation in which we let attachment drop away (*Gelassenheit*). Even monastic vows must be let go if they stand between seekers and their goal. At first glance, this seems in direct contrast to Krishna's caution that acts of sacrifice "...almsgiving and austerity should not be given up; their performance is necessary."[3] However, Krishna mitigates this admonition by saying that these acts must be performed *without attachment*, in effect turning his initial warning 180 degrees, into the spirit with which Eckhart so confidently speaks. For Hindu Lord and Dominican friar alike, inner detachment must be perfected before the seeker—whether warrior chieftain or Christian nun—is ready to enjoy the blessings God so joyfully bestows on and in the soul.

Like Arjuna, Eckhart has a question, too, and with typical Meisterish cheek, has the answer ever ready on his lips. "Now I ask: 'What is the object of pure detachment?'" A yogi might respond with the classic reply, "Neti, neti...not this, not this." "My answer," Eckhart continues, "is that the object of pure detachment is neither *this* nor *that*. It rests on absolutely nothing..."

> ...and I will you why: pure detachment rests on the highest, and he is at his highest, in whom God can work all His will. But God cannot work all His will in all hearts, for, although God is almighty, He can only work where He finds readiness or creates it.[4]

This climate of readiness seldom occurs naturally in a mortal being. Krishna suggests that the three tendencies or *gunas* are at their mischief once again. Kinds of renunciation, happiness, determination, and conscience—very different entities all—can without exception be linked to the predominance of *sattwa, tamas,* and *rajas*. Only the *sattwa* proclivity is recommended, and that only if the seeker can snuff out desire and delight even in spiritual practice and good works. Nonetheless, one must develop one's abilities for one's natural work. Arjuna, born to the warrior caste, must fulfill his foreordained destiny

---

3.   *Gita*, trans. Prabhavananda and Isherwood, 159.
4.   Eckhart, "On Detachment," in *Sermons*, 3:125.

(as detached from his accomplishments as any samurai would have been years later in feudal Japan, instinctively at one with his sword in a harmony of perfect action).

While most likely not familiar with the Indian caste system and surely not conversant with the *gunas*, Eckhart too acknowledges that different persons have dissimilar "boiling points" in life and in ascent to spiritual perfection. "If you heat a baker's oven and put in it dough of oats, barley, rye and wheat, there is only one heat in the oven, but it does not have the same effect on the different kinds of dough, for one turns into fine bread, the second coarser, and the third coarser still. And that is not the fault of the heat," he explains, "it is due to the materials which are unlike. In the same way God does not work alike in all our hearts: He works as He finds readiness and receptivity." Our old friends "this and that" may occupy space where God would like to squat. Only by emptying ourselves of these pesky preoccupations can we become an empty dwelling that only God can fill.

Ever committed to conveying the highest truths to all people, no matter what their education or station, Eckhart uses other concrete examples in his attempt to explain what emptiness is all about. One is the wax tablet. When I write on a wax tablet, then whatever is written on that tablet will prevent me from writing further on it in the future. "...if I want to write, I must erase or destroy whatever is on the tablet, and the tablet is never so suitable for me to write on as when there is nothing on it," he concludes.[5]

The resulting clarity of mind and spirit, and the receptivity to the divine nature, make it inevitable for the seeker to follow instructions such as Krishna provides to Arjuna: "Mentally resign all your actions to me. Regard me as your dearest one. Know me to be your only refuge. Be united always in heart and consciousness with me."[6] In reply to the question, "What does God want?", Eckhart quotes the Bible: "In all things I seek rest." (Eccles. 24:11) "But nowhere is perfect trust to be found," he states, "but in a detached heart."[7] *We must discard everything that suggests distinction or dualism.*[8] As the Son put on human nature, in Eckhart's theology, we in turn accept the divine nature. While men and women are not themselves God or gods, in essence—in the ground of their being—union with the Absolute occurs eternally as a continu-

5.   Ibid., 3:126.
6.   *Gita*, 171.
7.   Eckhart, 3:127..
8.   Eckhart, Sermon 47, *Sermons*, 2:28.

ous birth, streaming into the soul as light. "The Lord lives in the heart of every creature," states Krishna. "He turns them round and round upon the wheel of his *Maya*. Take refuge in him utterly. By his grace, you will find supreme peace, and the state which is beyond all change."[9]

Neither in the *Gita* nor in the sermons of Eckhart do we find the harping on mortification, wrestling with devils, or need to violently subdue the flesh so common in the monastic traditions of both Hinduism and Christianity until relatively recent times. In hammering time and again on the need for renunciation, Krishna advocates a healthy detachment toward the things that perish and immersion in a life of active devotion to the eternal God. Eckhart is positively rhapsodic in his single-minded focus on union as our birthright. Joy radiates from the pages that preserve his words for the ages. The negativism that both Eastern thought and mystics such as Eckhart have been accused of is a double-negative that cancels itself out. By erasing the writing, however fine, on the wax tablet, we gain the *tabula rasa*, the blank slate that God and humanity together inscribe in the same Hand. And so the quicker "…a man flees from the created, the quicker the Creator runs toward him,"[10] runs to him rejoicing, "just as if one were to turn a horse loose in a green meadow that was entirely smooth and level, and it would be the horse's nature to let himself go with all his strength in galloping about the meadow—he would enjoy it for it is his nature."[11]

And so Krishna's parting words echo through time as he places his arm in blessing around Arjuna's broad shoulders and declares,

> Give me your whole heart,
> Love and adore me,
> Worship me always,
> Bow to me only,
> And you shall find:
> This is my promise,
> Who love you dearly.
>
> Lay down all duties
> In me, your refuge.
> Fear no longer,

---

9. *Gita*, 172.
10. Eckhart, 3:128.
11. Eckhart, Sermon 57, *Sermons*, 2:86.

For I will save you
From sin and from bondage.[12]

For a person established in God's will wants nothing that is not God's will, Eckhart avers. It is a simple thing, to let God's love rule within. A person who does so is free, for the self has been left behind and is open to the blessing that will rush in as surely as air into a vacuum, or color into the darkness of the eye, for...

The eye with which I see God is the same eye with which God sees me: my eye and God's eye are one eye, one seeing, one knowing, and one love.[13]

Despite the enormity of their differences, here the author of the *Gita* and Meister Eckhart are on common ground across time and space, their essential message one of unity and consonance. "Whoever would attain perfect detachment should strive for perfect humility, and thus he will come to the neighborhood of God," Eckhart says at the conclusion of *On Detachment.*. "That this may be all our lot, so help us the highest detachment, which is God Himself. Amen."

---

12. *Gita*, 172.
13. Eckhart, Sermon 57, *Sermons*, 2:87.

The Not-So-Final Chapter

The Dominican friar Henry Suso (ca. 1300-1366) had a vision, and in that vision, his beloved mentor Meister Eckhart, who had been dead for several years, appeared before him. The Meister reported that he lived in "overflowing glory in which his soul had been made utterly god-like in God."[1] In answer to Suso's questions, the Meister said it was impossible to communicate in words how people who had lived lives of detachment and devotion to truth were "taken within the limitless abyss."[2]

When Suso asked the best way to live in order to attain this state, Eckhart answered, "Such a person should, with respect to his 'selfhood,' withdraw from himself in deep detachment and should receive all things from God and not from creatures, and should adopt an attitude of calm patience toward all wolf-ish men."[3] This last reference seems to refer to the inquisitors who made Eckhart's last months on earth a time of torment and humiliation.

Whether or not the Meister actually did communicate with Suso from "beyond the grave," the story is a sweet one and is consonant with what we know about Eckhart's life in pursuit of truth. I like to think of the Meister, enrobed in a soft, otherworldly glow, whispering the secrets of the spiritual life to the emotionally volatile Suso in the latter's small, dark cell. Suso doesn't tell us what language the Meister used, but I expect it was the Thuringian Middle High German of the sermons and treatises: a language of equals, and of intimacy. It is likely that Suso, a Dominican since his adolescence, had heard the

---

1.   Henry Suso, "The Life of the Servant," in *The Exemplar*, Classics of Western Spirituality, trans. Frank Tobin (New York: Paulist Press, 1989), 75.
2.   Ibid.
3.   Ibid.

Meister preach and was familiar with his mystical theology. Indeed, Eckhart, Suso, and (Johannes) Tauler, another Dominican, constitute the triumvirate of the male Rhineland mystical tradition in the late Middle Ages. What an experience to hear (or imagine) a message from another world where the Meister's teachings of relinquishment, total abandonment of the self to God, and calm tolerance for human frailty lived on in eternal truth!

At the conclusion this journey through the *Gita*, we, too, may feel that we have been blessed by an unexpected visitor. The Meister revealed through the lens of the *Bhagavad Gita* is not the same as the Eckhart of traditional scholarship or of disembodied quotations interpreted out of context.

One of the challenges to both scholarly and popular representations has been the difficulty of structuring the Meister's work in an exact chronology. Eckhart's work often was copied from memory by admirers, but much of it has been lost or was destroyed by people whose sensibilities he offended. This is most frustrating to those of us afflicted by what Alan Watts called "the classification sickness," the desire to label and brand everything and put it in alphabetical order in a neat, shiny box. We crave benchmarks and timelines to give meaning to a thinker's work. We seek to trace the development of certain ideas and identify *where* a new idea came into being.

Eckhart does not allow us to do this. A scholar attempting an overview of the Meister's output faces many roadblocks and questions. What *is* an authentic Eckhartian sermon or tract, a puzzle that has by no means been resolved despite more than 150 years of significant scholarly inroads. Then there is the question of audience. To whom were these words addressed? And when? Under what circumstances? When the questions distract from the content itself, the *Gita* serves as a way to focus and understand.

The *Gita* provides a sound, reliable structure through which we may study the Dominican's works, always pulling us back to the realization that many of Eckhart's key concepts are *universal* truths. The diffused influence of Platonism and the Eastern Church teachers alone would not be enough to account for these similarities and parallels. Surely, Eckhart tapped something eternally deep and true in his own experience as well as in his significant scholarly endeavors. Realizing this is a kind of small *satori* (instantaneous enlightenment) of its own for any who, at least on occasion, choose to filter his teachings through the *Gita*'s clarifying lens.

At the same time, by using the *Gita* as a lens, we may develop a more profound understanding of the *Gita* itself. How often have we dipped sporadically into its wisdom without regarding it as a cohesive whole, delighting in the trees but utterly missing out on the forest they create. In this new context, as the *Gita* is peeled back chapter by chapter, like the skin of a translucent onion, we may find greater depth, solid logic, spectacular poetry, and intellectual continuity far beyond our expectations. The *Gita* proves not simply an organizing device, but more importantly, an explicating force. The process may leave us almost as dazzled and put-in-our-place as Arjuna after he gets his wish to see God's glory. (One can almost imagine the exasperated Krishna, fed up with the clueless one's nattering, saying, "OK, you want to see God? Well, don't tell me I didn't warn you. *This* is God!")

What do we know about Meister Eckhart that we didn't know before? Certainly, the factual information is the same. He is still the Dominican "Paris Master" (with the twinkle in his eye), and the preacher with a penchant for shocking us out of our complacency. But his celebrated "negative theology" feels much less onerous now. Images of darkness, the desert, the abyss seem to suggest a state we can't express in words, rather than to define a world bereft of color, light, or life. Because we've viewed him through a gospel of another religion and culture, Eckhart now seems even more universal, a man for all seasons of religious diversity and pluralism. And paradoxically (a word uniquely suited to the Meister), he is someone who believes in tradition and the teachings of his Church no matter how radical his words, how self-actualized his own journey to the light. In fact, it could be said that Eckhart used the Church as a lens to penetrate Reality much as we have used the *Gita* to closely scrutinize the work of the Dominican master.

By viewing Eckhart through the *Gita*, a number of important points have been established. There are striking commonalities between both texts especially in regard to the existence of the *Ground* (*Brahman*) and the paths that lead to realization (e.g., work, knowledge, practices, detachment from the fruits of one's labor, love, meditation and faith). By viewing Eckhart in this exceptional manner one can clearly see the amazing similarities between the Hindu perspective that *Brahman* (Self) is *Atman* (self), and Eckhart's contention that there is a place in the soul which is of the same substance as the Godhead.

Eckhart's view that God is in all things mirrors Krishna's contention that God pervades the universe. The *Gita's* teaching that there are paths that surely lead to the divine, but that even these paths must be abandoned, reflects Eckhart's admonition that monks and nuns will have to give up even their vows and their attachment to *ideas* about God if they would get beyond the idea and seize the essence, the dance of life. For the Lord of the Dance is a motif in both Hindu and Christian traditions. Shiva is depicted as the dancing god. In Christianity, C.S. Lewis is part of a long, honorable tradition when he calls God's plan "the Great Dance" in his novel, *Perelandra*. God dances through Eckhart, sometimes as a frisky colt romping in the meadow of the soul.

At the same time, the striking differences between Hinduism and Christianity remain, providing diversity for us to ponder and appreciate. For example, Krishna speaks of reincarnation for those who do not attain the highest in this life. For Eckhart, there is no *physical* rebirth, only the birth of the Word in the ground of the soul, and that is a continuous awakening outside of time and place.

In retrospect, I feel that viewing Eckhart through the *Gita* has greatly enlarged my understanding of the medieval mystic as well as one of the most eloquent Hindu testaments. The methodology of using a scriptural text from one tradition to view the ideas of a thinker from another culture and time is surprisingly effective in providing a fresh perspective and helping us focus on what Aldous Huxley called "The Perennial Philosophy" underlying the world's great spiritual pathways. Using this technique, world religions can look through the lens of "The Other" to shed light on their own convictions and beliefs (and grow to appreciate a different perspective in the bargain).

In conclusion, M. O'C. Walshe, the eminent Middle High German scholar and translator of the vernacular sermons and treatises into English, offers a grace note of his own in the form of a disputed work known as "The Master's Final Words." While this text is not entirely authenticated, it may in fact represent the Meister's last words to his followers before he set off for Avignon the year before his death, according to Walshe.[4] In some ways, the Meister's final advice offers an appropriate recapitulation to a theme and variations that has allowed two diverse mystical traditions to reveal to us their own harmonious counterpoint:

> Now see. In whatever way you find God most, and you are most often aware of Him, that is the way you should follow. But if another way presents itself, quite contrary to the first, and if, having abandoned the first way, you find God as much in the new way as in the one that you have left, then that is right. But the noblest and

---

4. M. O'C. Walshe, *Meister Eckhart: Sermons & Treatises, Vol. III*, Introduction, Longmead, Shaftsbury: Element Books Ltd., 1987, 7.

best thing would be this, if a man were come to such equality, with such calm and certainty that he could find God and enjoy Him in any way and in all things, without having to wait for anything or chase after anything: that would delight me! For this, and to this end all works are done, and every work helps towards this. If anything does not help towards this, you should let it go.[5]

Once again and for the last time, Eckhart declares that God is in all modes, and equally accessible in all modes, for the person who can take Him equally.[6] Whether for Hindu warrior, medieval monk, or a modern sojourner on the spiritual quest, surely this maxim is the seed of a universal dance whose echo may never end.

5.   Ibid., 148.
6.   Ibid., 147.

APPENDIX

Unitive Consciousness:
A Universal Theme

To rise above plurality and to descend deeply into the unitive state, and to remain there eternally, is a desire understood and supported by most of the world's great religious traditions, at least in some of their manifestations. The following statements and quotations attest to the presence of the belief in unitive consciousness in six major traditions:

Buddhism: In Buddhism, the devotee clears the mind of distractions through frequent meditation, until the state of union known as nirvana is achieved. Sogyal Rinpoche, a Tibetan lama, wrote: "When you live in the wisdom home, you'll no longer find a barrier between 'I' and 'you,' 'this' and 'that,' 'inside' and 'outside;' you'll have come, finally, to your true home, the state of non-duality."[1]

Christianity: Jesus told his disciples, "Neither pray I for these alone, but for them also which shall believe on me through the word; That they all may be one; as thou, Father, art in me, and I in thee, that they also may be one in us: that the world may believe that thou hast sent me. And the glory which thou gavest me I have given them; that they may be one, even as we are one: I in them, and thou in me, that they may be made perfect in one; and that the world may know that thou hast sent me, and hast loved them, as thou hast loved me." (John 17:20-23)

---

1. Sogyal Rinpoche. *The Tibetan Book of Living and Dying.* New York: HarperCollins Publishers, Inc., 1993, 77.

Hinduism: Vedanta, one of the six schools of Hinduism, holds that we perceive the duality between self and Self because of *maya*, sort of a systemwide illusion that permeates the phenomenal world. By stilling the mind and practicing yogas, the seeker attains *samadhi*, Self realization.

Islam: Attar, a Sufi mystic, wrote, "Caught in the spell of His love's ecstasy/ Immerse yourself for evermore, O mind/In Him who is Pure Knowledge and Pure Bliss."[2]

Judaism: Study of the Kabbalah has long provided a rich source of mystical inspiration to practitioners of Judaism. According to Abulafia, "For now he (the mystic) is no longer separated from his Master, and behold he is his Master and his Master is he; for he is so intimately united with Him, that he cannot by any means be separated from Him, for he is He…"[3]

Taoism: "Be aware of all that is, and dwell in the Infinite," wrote Chuang Tzu.[4]

---

2.   Attar, quoted in *The Element Book of Mystical Verse*, ed. Alan Jacobs, (Rockport, Mass: Element Books Limited, 1997), 61

3.   Abraham Abulafia, quoted by Moshe Idel, *Studies in Ecstatic Kabbalah*, (Albany: State University of New York Press, 1988), 10.

4.   Chuang Tzu, *Inner Chapters*, (New York: Vintage Books/Random House, 1974), 159.

Bibliography

Note: The standard edition of Meister Eckhart's work in Latin and German is *Die deutschen und lateinischen Werke*, Stuttgart and Berlin: Verlag W. Kohlhammer, 11 Vols., 1936 , still in progress. The German works (DW) were edited by Josef Quint, the Latin (LW) by Ernst Benz and a team of scholars.

Besant, Annie Wood, trans. *Bhagavad Gita.* Wheaton, Ill.: The Theosophical Publishing House, 1914.

Blakney, Raymond B. *Meister Eckhart.* New York: Harper Torchbooks, Harper & Row, 1941.

Clark, James M. *Meister Eckhart.* London: Thomas Nelson and Sons Ltd., 1957.

Davies, Oliver. *Meister Eckhart: Mystical Theologian.* London: SPCK, 1991.

_____. *Meister Eckhart: Selected Writings*, London, New York: Penguin Books, 1994.

_____. *The Rhineland Mystics*, New York: Spiritual Classics, Crossroad, 1989.

Ghose, Aurobindo, ed. *Bhagavad Gita and Its Message.* Twin Lakes, Wisconsin: Lotus Light Publications, 1995. Reissue of the 1938 original.

Gnaneswarananda, Swami. *Yoga for Beginners.* Chicago: Vivekananda Vedanta Press, 1975.

Holt, Linda. *Threads of Yoga: The Yoga Sutras of Patanjali*, California State University-Dominguez Hills, 1993.

Kelley, Carl Franklin. *Meister Eckhart on Divine Knowledge*. New Haven: Yale University Press, 1977.

Kern, Udo. *Die Anthropologie des Meister Eckhart*. Hamburg: Verlag Dr. Kovac, 1994.

Largier, Niklaus. *Meister Eckhart Werke I*. Frankfurt am Main: Deutscher Klassiker Verlag, 1993.

_____. *Meister Eckhart Werke II*, Frankfurt am Main: Deutscher Klassiker Verlag, 1993.

Lomperis, Timothy J. *Hindu Influence on Greek Philosophy*. Calcutta, India: Minerva Associates Pvt. Ltd., 1984.

McGinn, Bernard, ed. *Meister Eckhart, Vol. 1*. New York, Mahwah, Toronto: Classics of Western Spirituality, Paulist Press, 1981.

_____. *Meister Eckhart and the Beguine Mystics*. New York: Continuum, 1994.

_____. *Meister Eckhart, Teacher and Preacher*, Vol. 2. New York, Mahwah, Toronto: Classics of Western Spirituality, Paulist Press, 1986.

_____. *The Mystical Thought of Meister Eckhart*. New York: Crossroad Publishing, 2001.

Milne, Joseph, "Eckhart and the Problem of Christian Non-Dualism: A Comparative Study of Eckhart and Advaita Vedanta," *The Eckhart Review 6* (March 1993).

Nikhilananda, Swami, trans. *Bhagavad Gita,*. New York: Ramakrishna-Vivekananda Center, 1944.

Prabhavananda, Swami, and Christopher Isherwood, ed. and trans., *How to Know God: The Yoga Aphorisms of Patanjali*, Hollywood: Vedanta Press, 1971 (sixth printing).

_____. *The Song of God: Bhagavad-Gita*, Hollywood: Vedanta Press, 1969.

Schmidt, K. O. (Karl Otto). *Meister Eckhart's Way to Cosmic Consciousness: A Breviary of Practical Mysticism*. Lakemont: CSA Press, 1976.

Schürmann, Reiner. *Meister Eckhart, Mystic and Philosopher: Translations with Commentary*. Bloomington: Indiana University Press, 1978.

Shah-Kazemi, Reza. "Transcendence and Immanence: Common Themes in Eckhart, Shankara and Ibn Arabi," *The Eckhart Review 6* (Spring 1997).

Smith, Cyprian. *The Way of Paradox: Spiritual Life as Taught by Meister Eckhart*. New York: Paulist Press, 1987.

Smith, Huston. *The World's Religions*. San Francisco: HarperSanFrancisco, 1991. Revised and updated edition of *Religions of Man*, 1958.

Underhill, Evelyn. *Practical Mysticism*. Mineola, N.Y.: Dover Publications, Inc., 2000. Originally published by E. P. Dutton & Co., New York, 1915.

Walshe, M.O'C. *Meister Eckhart, Sermons & Treatises, Vol. I*. Longmead, Shaftsbury: Element Books Ltd., 1987.

_____. Meister Eckhart, *Sermons & Treatises, Vol. 2*. Longmead, Shaftsbury: Element Books Ltd., 1987.

_____. Meister Eckhart, *Sermons & Treatises, Vol. 3*, Longmead, Shaftsbury: Element Books Ltd., 1987.

Weeks, Andrews. *German Mysticism from Hildegard of Bingen to Ludwig Wittgenstein*. Albany: State University of New York Press, 1993.

Wolz-Gottwald, Eckard. *Meister Eckhart und die klassischen Upanishaden.* Würzburg: Koenigshausen und Neumann, 1984.

Woods, Richard, O.P. *Eckhart's Way.* Wilmington: Michael Glazier, 1986.

Glossary

Abgescheidenheit—Detachment, used by Meister Eckhart to suggest the active process of distancing oneself from everything that is not God. (See also *Detachment* and *Gelassenheit.)*

Avatar—According to believers in a number of faith traditions, the incarnation of God or a god in human form.

Avidya—In Hinduism, the ignorance that keeps us from knowing the Reality beyond appearances.

Beguines—Beginning in the 12th century in Netherlands and spreading through western Europe in the Middle Ages, communities of unmarried women who took no vows, but lived lives devoted to God and followed a path of poverty, chastity, self-employment, and good works. Although these communities did not have the approval of the Church, some of the most celebrated women theologians of the Middle Ages were *Beguines*, notably Mechthild of Magdeburg, Beatrice of Nazareth, Hadewijch of Brabant, and Marguerite Porete.

Detachment—The process of remaining emotionally distanced from the senses and everyday life in order to focus one's attention more fully on the divine.

Dominicans—The Roman Catholic religious order founded by St. Dominic in the 13th century whose mission is to preach and save souls, according to its Constitutions.

Dualism—(From Latin *duo*, two). 1). the religious or theological system which would explain the universe as the outcome of two eternally opposed and coexisting principles, conceived as good and evil, light and darkness, or some other form of conflicting powers. 2). the ordinary view that the existing universe contains two radically distinct kinds of being or substance—matter and spirit, body and mind. This is the most frequent use of the name in modern philosophy, where it is commonly contrasted with monism.[1]

Gelassenheit—In Meister Eckhart, detachment as a passive "letting go" of attachment to the senses and the phenomenal world. (See also *Abgescheidenheit* and *Detachment.*)

Ground (Grund in German or *grunt* in Middle High German)—The undifferentiated Source from which all Being flows. The Godhead (as opposed to God who may wear a personal, knowable face). The Ground of the Soul is that uncreated part of the soul which is of the same substance as the Ground of Being. In the Ground of the Soul, the individual may experience union with the divine.

Implend—The author's neologism created to complement the verb "transcend." As "transcend" indicates going beyond through external projection, "implend" suggests sinking beneath introspection.

Homoousion—(Greek for "same substance). Of one and the same substance. The word was used by the Council of Nicea (325 C.E.) in affirming that Christ's nature was both fully human and fully divine. It also applies to the orthodox Christian view of the three persons of the Trinity: different as persons (*hypostasis*) but the same in substance (*homoousion*).[2]

Hypostatic Union—Union of essential nature. *Hypostasis* means that which lies beneath as basis or foundation. In Greek philosophy (i.e., Aristotle), reality as distinguished from appearances. In Christian theology, hypostatic union refers specifically to the Incarnation (Christ) as one person subsisting in two natures (divine and human).[3]

Interpenetration—In Orthodox Christian theology, the process whereby two or more aspects of being inform each other simultaneously. For example, the

---

1.   *The Catholic Encyclopedia, http://*www.newadvent.org./
2.   Ibid.
3.   Ibid.

human and divine natures of Christ would be said to interpenetrate each other.

Kinesis—(From the Greek, *kinsis*, movement, from *kinein*, to move) Movement or activity of an organism in response to a stimulus such as light.[4]

Koan—A verbal puzzle or illogical sound or statement given to a student of Rinzai Zen Buddhism in order to facilitate meditation. Rinzai Zen students concentrate on koans until their conventional thinking cracks, and they break through into enlightenment.

Monism—(From the Greek *monos*, "one", "alone", "unique"). A philosophical term which, in its various meanings, is opposed to dualism or pluralism. Wherever pluralistic philosophy distinguishes a multiplicity of things, Monism denies that the manifoldness is ultimately real, and holds that the apparently many are temporal phases, or phenomena, of a final one.[5]

Mysticism—(From *myein*, to initiate). A religious tendency and spiritual desire of the human soul towards intimate union with the Divine, or a system growing out of such a tendency and desire.[6] The art of union with Reality.[7]

Nous—Greek term for mind, reason, or intellect.

Ontological Arguments—Arguments from analytic, *a priori* or necessary premises to the conclusion that God exists.[8] Because this is a particularly subtle concept, I quote the following example of an ontological argument from the *Stanford Encyclopedia of Philosophy*:

4. *American Heritage® Dictionary of the English Language*, Fourth Edition, Copyright © 2000 by Houghton Mifflin Company.
5. Ibid.
6. Ibid.
7. Evelyn Underhill, *Practical Mysticism*, Mineola, N.Y.: Dover Publications, Inc., 2000, reprinted from the 1915 E. P. Dutton & Co., Inc., edition.
8. Copyright © 1996 by Graham Oppy, Monash University. *Stanford Encyclopedia of Philosophy*, http://plato.stanford.edu/entries/ontological-arguments/#Hist

(An early example is from) St. Anselm of Canterbury in the 11th century C.E. In his *Proslogion*, St. Anselm claims to derive the existence of God from the concept of *a being than which no greater can be conceived*. St. Anselm reasoned that, if such a being fails to exist, then a greater being—namely, a being than which no greater can be conceived, and which exists—can be conceived. But this would be absurd: nothing can be greater than a being than which no greater can be conceived. So a being than which no greater can be conceived—i.e., God—exists.

Ontological Union—A union of essence, substance or being. This is *absolute* union in which the entities uniting lose their individual properties. In mysticism, the substantive union of divine and human.

Pantheism—(From Greek *pan*, all; *theos*, god). The view according to which God and the world are one[9] (and therefore the same). In this view, all things are divine.

Panentheism—(From the Greek, all-in-god). The author uses this term to express the view that God permeates all things, yet transcends or is "more real than" the phenomenal world. The term was coined by Charles Hartshorne (1897-2000), an American philosopher. According the on-line *Stanford Encyclopedia of Philosophy*, Hartshorne's *panentheism* holds that everything that exists "is in the one God by means of omniscience and omnibenevolence. All creaturely feelings, especially feelings of suffering, are included in the divine life. God is seen by Hartshorne as the mind or soul for the whole body of the natural world, although he thinks of God as distinguishable from the creatures."[10] The on-line *Dictionary of Modern Western Theology* states that Hartshorne's panentheism "is intended to express the idea that everything in the world is immediately experienced by God and that God responds to the world

---

9.   *Catholic Encyclopedia.*
10. Copyright © 2001 by Dan Dombrowski, *Stanford Encyclopedia of Philosophy*, http://plato.stanford.edu/entries/hartshorne/

so that every part of it experiences the consequences of divine choice. But God is not identifiable with the world."[11]

Samsara—In Buddhism and Hinduism, the eternal cycle of birth, life, and death.

Self—Used in two senses in Vedanta. The phenomenal *self* experiences life dualistically, drawing a sharp distinction between the individual and the Divine. In this usage, the *self* may worship God as the "Other." The *Self* represents a non-dualistic perspective in which universal Divine and individual soul are the same substance. In this usage, the individual, through meditation, comes to a realization that *self* and *Self* are one. In the Patristic Christian tradition, *self*-emptying (*kenosis*) is necessary before one can experience the unity of the *Self*.

Soul—The essence of being. "…the ultimate internal principle by which we think, feel, and will, and the spirit and life force by which our physical bodies are animated. The term *nous* usually denotes this principle as the subject of our conscious states, while *soul* denotes the source of our vegetative activities as well."[12]

---

11. *Dictionary of Modern Western Theology,* Boston University, http://people.bu.edu/wwildman/WeirdWildWeb/courses/mwt/dictionary/mwt_themes_842_hartshorne.htm
12. *Catholic Encyclopedia.*

0-595-32492-4